AF653116

American Women Novelists

A Feminist Interpretation of the Role of the Male Protagonist in the Novels of

Edith Wharton
Ellen Glasgow &
Willa Cather

To

Mummy & Papa
for
their constant support and encouragement
and unflinching faith in me

American Women Novelists

A Feminist Interpretation of the
Role of the Male Protagonist
in the Novels of

Edith Wharton
Ellen Glasgow &
Willa Cather

Rajyashree Khushu-Lahiri

PRESTIGE

Published by
PRESTIGE BOOKS
3/28, East Patel Nagar
New Delhi 110 008

© Author
2000

ISBN: 81-7551-092-7

Composed by Vivek Mathur, Delhi 110 006 Ph. 3981867
Printed at Chaman Offset Press, New Delhi 110 002

Contents

Introduction
7

The Negative Hero:
Edith Wharton's Male Protagonist
25

The Polygamous Male:
Ellen Glasgow's Protagonist
66

The Little Male: Willa Cather's Protagonist
95

Conclusion
125

Bibliography
134

Acknowledgements

I would first like to express my sincere gratitude to Professor R.K. Gupta for inspiring me to take up the present project. His insistence that my project was entirely my own affair, instilled in me the necessary confidence to pursue research independently thereafter.

During the process of revising and updating this book, the ASRC has been very prompt with providing reference material.

I must also make a special mention of Mr. Pandurangan, for his meticulous typing and cooperation.

As for my sons, Abhik and Pratik, their questions and comments stemming from innocent curiosity, although exasperating at times, yet encouraged me to go ahead.

And last but not the least, Somu for his implicit faith and trust in me.

Introduction

In a famous letter to Charlotte Bronte, Robert Southey expressed the idea that "Literature is not the business of a woman's life and it cannot be."[1] The notion that, because they are by definition male activities, reading, writing and thinking are not only alien but inimical to the female self was widely accepted in the nineteenth century.

The three writers included in this study, Edith Wharton, Ellen Glasgow and Willa Cather, grew to creative maturity in a society which subscribed to such values and each in her own way had to overcome obstacles in order to gain acceptance as an artist. These three writers can be grouped together because they are linked by gender, class, race, intellectual and socio-cultural milieu, ideological environment, literary tradition and period. Further, each one of them was a prolific writer of fiction. All of them lived beyond the age of seventy and devoted ripened powers to a vocation that had absorbed them from youth. All three had descended from ancestors who had been Americans for generations, and shared the influence of Anglicanism as a shaping force. More importantly, all three testify to an engrossing feminism, in particular, assimilationist feminism, that came to the forefront in the early years of the twentieth century. Earlier, during the nineteenth century, feminist theory had included two separate ideological currents—the liberal (which was essentially assimilationist) and the cultural. The liberal tradition, which was rooted in Enlightenment liberal premises, maintained that men and women are ontologically similar and hence women should be accorded equal access to the male dominated public sphere. Further, it advocated that women should acquire the traits traditionally associated with men; reason, coolness and ambition. Wharton, Cather and Glasgow were writing in the heyday of assimilationist feminism and they were deeply influenced by it. Further, it is interesting to note that though these women wrote in different regions of America, had different cultural backgrounds and did not know one another, they show marked similarity in the treatment of the male protagonists, specifically in the way these male protagonists relate with the female protagonists. It is in this aspect of their novels that the working of the "female sensibility" is perhaps, most apparent. A detailed analysis of the novels included in this study will reveal that these novelists wrote from a distinctively female perspective arising out of their complex cultural position.

Until recent years women writers were accorded relatively brief coverage in the standard literary histories. In many of the major critical studies designed to explore the essential spirit and style of a particular literary period or of the national literature as a whole, they either received much less emphasis than males or were completely ignored. When women writers were discussed they were forced into limiting categories. However, a number of feminist scholars, chief among them Mary Ellmann in *Thinking About Women*, have demonstrated that in the past, literature by women was often misread and misunderstood because certain presuppositions about female talent were so pervasive that they began to be considered accurate descriptions of women's writing. Earlier critics (who were generally male) had a tendency to project and expand their own culture-bound stereotypes of femininity. Some of the recurring stereotypes that have been identified are that women writers typically exhibit excessive reliance on autobiography, have the habit of focussing on trivial subject matter, and operate from intuitive rather than analytic sensibility. These feminist scholars have argued that many earlier critics were reluctant to speak of women writers without reference to their sex not because they feared that women might create a separate, different and equally significant literature, but because they were convinced that women's writings were inherently less important than men's.

In the last two decades, the American literary tradition has been subjected to a revision aimed at including female perspectives. Women writers have been rigorously reexamined and their contribution to the understanding of the female experience has been highlighted. The attempt to provide better conceptual frameworks for the study of women writers has inevitably involved these scholars in the longstanding and as yet unresolved debate about whether and to what extent the consciousness of being a woman affects the workings of the literary imagination. Some critics contend that the whole question of sex should be considered irrelevant in literary studies because the characteristics of a true writer are originality of style and uniqueness of vision, the function of the critic being to illuminate these. Others, sensing a distinctively female voice and vision in literature by women, have, on the other hand, maintained that fictional language, structure and content are at least in part determined by the sex of the creator. Although they have avoided sweeping generalizations about the nature of the female mind, these scholars have yet continued to search for evidence of a demonstrable relationship between creativity and gender. Through their rigorous reexaminations of groups of women writers, these scholars have tried to answer some vexing questions such as, whether these writers have been possessed of a strong awareness of themselves as women, whether they have developed a literary tradition different from men's, and whether their works invariably, albeit sometimes covertly, contain discourses about the situations of women in their contemporary worlds. By and large, most scholars would concur with Elaine Showalter that when works by women writers are considered collectively "we can see an imaginative continuum, the recurrence of certain patterns, themes, problems, and images from generation to generation."[2] Thus a distinct female literary tradition may be traced which is different from, though not necessarily inferior to, the male literary tradition. A rapid glance at the volume of literature produced on this subject will indicate the importance of the issue under consideration. However, as it is not possible to deal with the entire body of writing on the subject, I shall briefly discuss some of the more representative works.

That women writers present a different point of view from that of men writers, was first pointed out by George Henry Lewes in 1852, when he said:

> The advent of female literature promises woman's view of life, woman's experience: in other words, a new element. Make what distinctions you please in the social world, it still remains true that men and women have different organizations, consequently different experiences. . . . But hitherto . . . the literature of women has fallen short of its functions owing to a very natural and a very explicable weakness—it has been too much a literature of imitation. To write as men write is the aim and besetting sin of women: to write as women is the real task they have to perform.[3]

George Eliot took a somewhat similar stand when she insisted that distinctively feminine conditions must give rise to distinctive forms and combinations.

Writing about women and fiction Virginia Woolf speculated that perhaps "the nerves that feed the brain would seem to differ in men and women."[4] Values and experiences of women differ greatly from those of men and yet it is the masculine values that prevail.

According to Mrs. Woolf, due to this, and to the fact that they had no literary tradition behind them, a woman novelist of the early nineteenth century was "often caught in the double bind of admitting that she was 'only a woman,' or protesting that she was 'as good as a man.'"[5] She also hoped that women would some day, develop a literary style of their own which would be shaped out of their own needs and for their own uses, and that there would emerge a feminine style expressive of a unique female mind.

Patricia Meyer Spacks, who has devoted an entire book to the subject of the "female imagination" claims that "a special female self-awareness emerges through literature in every period."[6] It is certainly not a fact that books written by women necessarily differ from books by men, as women also deal with the perennial problems that have concerned novelists through the centuries, such as relationships, personal identity, and the interchange between individual and society. Yet, she insists, "there seems to be something that we might call a woman's point of view . . . a vague enough phenomenon, doubtless the result mainly of social conditioning, but an outlook sufficiently distinct to be recognizable through the centuries."[7] For certain historical reasons which can be easily discerned women writers have "characteristically concerned themselves with matters more or less peripheral to male concerns."[8] To this may be attributed the inevitable differences in the literary emphases and subject matters of female and male writers. In her survey of prose, fiction and autobiography by women in the Anglo-American tradition over the last three centuries, Spacks individuates a number of frequently recurring themes and issues. Chief among them are the conflict between passivity and moral growth, the problems of altruism and of taking care of other people, the psychological effects of social conditioning on female adolescents, and the complex motives that underlie the woman's choice of the artist's role. Further, she asserts that few generalizations can be made about the forms and techniques of women's writing, but many about women's problems. "Through all literary genres criticism as well as poetry, fiction, autobiography—women demonstrate their approaches to the solving of those problems. The same consciousness of difficulty presents itself over and over."[9]

Annette Kolodny in her attempt to define feminist literary criticism addresses herself to the problem of whether "there *is* something unique about women's writing."[10] She contends that so far what women have expressed in literature is what they have been *able to express*. This, according to her, is a consequence of "the complex interplay between innate biological determinants, personal and individual talents, opportunities, and the larger effects of socialization, which, in some cases, may govern the limits of expression or even of perceptions and experience itself."[11] She further points out that in every society there are accepted rules of discourse which often vary for men and women and these too will affect the parameters of what may or may not be spoken or revealed. The fact that women experience the world differently from men and that they often write out of that different and sometimes "other" perspective of experience has become virtually a truism in feminist critical circles. A close examination of a sampling of contemporary women writers in the United States has revealed clearly demonstrable repetitions of thematic concerns, image patterns, and stylistic devices among these authors. For example, these writers often endow their female characters with "reflective perceptions," a habit of mind which becomes a repeated stylistic device, as one after the other, each character is depicted discovering herself or finding some part of herself in activities she has not planned, or in situations she cannot fully comprehend.

Another phenomenon that often occurs in women's writing is what Kolodny calls "inversion," which operates in a number of complex ways. On the one hand, the stereotyped, traditional literary images of women are being turned around to reveal either their inherent absurdity, or their hidden reality, though in new ways. On the other hand, there is a tendency to "invert" more generalized traditional images and conventional associations so that they come to connote their opposites. Often, all the nice comfortable associations of a previous (mostly male dominated) literary tradition are overthrown. Love is revealed as violence; suicide and death are imaged as comforting and attractive, while loneliness and violence become, for their heroines, means to self-knowledge and contentment. The "inversion" pattern at times even structures the plot. Our conventional expectations of a happy ending are denied, and in its place is substituted a conventionally unhappy ending, which nevertheless, in terms of the particular work, pleases and satisfies us. Thus, "what may appear as impossibly freaky or neurotic at first reading is, in reality, the tentative process of discovering—in literary terms—what the world looks and feels like to that segment of the population which is taught the 'only way . . . to control her future' is to 'choose her man.'"[12]

Vivian Gornick admits that there has been much thoughtful discussion on the question of the "female sensibility" and its compositional elements but feels that so far these complex questions have not been answered. She notes that the subjection of women has led to the fact that for centuries the cultural record of our experience has been a record of male experience. However, women also have their own cultural past and the femaleness of their experience is buried in this past. According to Gornick, in order to achieve wholeness, women "must become artists and analysands: they must break through to the center of their experience, and hold that experience upto the light of consciousness if their lives are to be transformed."[13] Like the growth of a genuinely experiencing woman, the growth of a genuine female sensibility is a generational task and will take a long time to evolve. At present in the works of women writers one rarely finds femaleness at the centre of the universe, and what it is to be a woman used effectively to reflect life metaphorically. However, there are works in which one can feel the heroic effort stirring—in which the writer seems to be groping magnificently for "her" sentence.

Gilbert and Gubar in their seminal study *The Madwoman in the Attic: The Woman Writer and the Nineteenth Century Literary Imagination* point out how the literary woman was always faced with equally degrading options when she had to define her public presence in the world. She could either modestly confess her female "limitations" and concentrate on the "lesser" subjects reserved for ladies as becoming to their inferior powers, or she could rebel and accept the inevitable ostracism. Often she was forced into publishing her work pseudonymously or anonymously. Highlighting the interrelations and tensions between literature by women and literature by men, Gilbert and Gubar explore how British and American women writers in the last century responded to the male literary traditions and to its images of women. Building on Harold Bloom's theory of the "anxiety of influence," which posits that truly creative artists are inevitably at odds with their literary predecessors, the authors maintain that before female writers in the Victorian age could assert themselves as artists, they had to confront the two "paradigmatic polarities—angel or monster—in terms of which earlier writers had depicted women." According to the authors, many female writers resolved this problem by revising or inverting these very images, transforming the monsters into madwomen who lashed out at patriarchal institutions, and the angels into heroines afflicted with limiting psychological problems. They further suggest that these writers used their angels or madwomen to express their own subversive desire to challenge social and literary conventions. "Indeed much of the poetry and fiction written by women conjures up this mad creature so that female authors can come to terms with their own uniquely female feelings of fragmentation, their own keen sense of the discrepancies between what they are and what they are supposed to be."[14] In short, women writers in the nineteenth century "produced literary works that are in some sense palimpsestic, works whose surface designs conceal or obscure deeper, less accessible (and less socially acceptable) levels of meaning. Thus these authors managed the difficult task of achieving true female literary authority by simultaneously conforming to and subverting patriarchal literary standards."[15] For example, one pattern that seems to be concealed in most of the writings by women is the woman writer's quest for her own story; in other words, the quest for self-definition. In addition, the imagery of entrapment which expresses "the woman writer's sense that she has been dispossessed precisely because she is so thoroughly posseessed"[16]; the imagery of enclosure which reflects the woman writer's sense of powerlessness and discomfort dominates the literature of both nineteenth century women and their twentieth century descendants.

According to Annis Pratt, "Women's fiction represents an experience radically different from men's because our drive towards growth as persons is thwarted by our society's prescriptions concerning gender . . . the tension between what Apollo intends and Daphne is willing to accept, between forces demanding our submissions and our rebellious assertions of personhood, characterize far too much of our fiction to be incidental."[17] In her study of women's fiction Pratt distinguishes many archetypal patterns such as the rape-trauma archetype, the green-world archetype, the growing-up-grotesque archetype.

The 1980 volume of *Women and Literature* was entitled *Gender and Literary Voice*, and as Janet Todd said in her introduction, it tried to answer the question "Is there a distinctive female style/tone/content?"[18] Although no definitive answer was provided, the various essays included in the volume examined works by British, French and American women writers, some emphasizing their distinctive style and tone, others their different content—what Joyce Carol Oates terms "Women's insights—women's very special adventures."[19]

A recent collection of essays entitled *Writing and Sexual Difference* has indicated the scope of feminist inquiry and examined "how writing relates to gender, how attitudes toward sexual difference generate and structure literary texts, and how critical methods can effectively disclose the traces of gender in literature."[20] It is only recently that this notion of difference has emerged as a focus of feminist criticism. Female experience has displaced male bias as the centre of analysis, as have female literary genealogies the male traditions. Literary studies have emphasized the distinctive features of female texts and have traced connecting lines which place women in a fertile, and, by and large, autonomous tradition.

Elaine Showalter in a penetrating essay entitled "Feminist Criticism in the Wilderness" coined the term "gynocritics" to describe the study of women as writers. Instead of adapting male models and theories the aim of gynocritics is to develop new models based on the study of female experience and to construct a female framework for the analysis of women's literature. This has become necessary as in the past decade or so, the process of defining the feminine has started to take place. She evaluates four theories of sexual difference in women's writing—biological, linguistic, psychological and cultural—and attempts to show that women's writing has its own unique character because it draws on female body images, uses a "woman's language," and expresses the female psyche.

Thus, she concludes, women's writing reflects their complex cultural position and so a model based on women's culture provides the most complete and satisfying way to explain the specificity and difference of women's writing. This model incorporates ideas about women's body, language and psyche, but interprets them in relation to the social contents in which they occur. The ways in which women conceptualize their bodies and their sexual and reproductive functions are closely related to their environment. The female psyche itself can be studied as the product of cultural forces, and linguistic behavior is also shaped by cultural ideals. It cannot be denied that there are important differences among women writers themselves: class, race, nationality, and history determine literary production as significantly as gender. Nevertheless, women's culture forms a collective experience within the cultural whole, and binds women writers to each other over time and space.

In defining female culture, it is essential to distinguish between the roles, activities, tastes and behaviors prescribed and considered appropriate for women, and the activities, behaviours and functions actually generated out of women's lives. In the nineteenth century the term "women's sphere" expressed the Victorian vision of separate roles for women and men with the women's role being subordinate. Although this notion of separate roles was defined and maintained by men, women often internalized its precepts in the "cult of true womanhood" and the "feminine ideal." Women's culture, however, redefines women's "activities and goals from a woman centered point of view. . . . The term implies an assertion of equality and an awareness of sisterhood, the commonality of women."[21] However, since women writers have lived and are living within the male-dominated society, they cannot be fully independent from its cultural, economic and political pressures. And so, women's writing may be termed a "double voiced discourse" which embodies the social, literary and cultural heritages of both the "muted" and the "dominant."[22]

The difference in women's writing, then, is to be understood only in terms of this complex historical and cultural tradition.

Historically, woman has been regarded as being in some sense inferior to man. According to Aristotle, "the male is by nature superior, and the female inferior; and the one rules and the other is ruled; this principle of necessity extends to all mankind."[23] St. Thomas pronounced woman to be an "imperfect man," an "incidental" being.[24] In *The Second Sex*, a pioneering study of woman and her historical and contemporary situation in Western culture, Simone de Beauvoir, a wide-ranging thinker with strong existentialist and feminist leanings, examines her subject matter from social, historical, biological, psychological, mythological, and literary standpoints. She contends that women's development as free and independent beings and their achievements in many of the endeavors they have undertaken have been impeded by the fact that they have generally been forced to occupy a secondary place in the world in relation to men. This occurred not due to any biologically imposed necessity but because of elaborate traditions, cultural patterns, and social structures firmly under the control of men. Thus, as de Beauvoir remarks, "humanity is male and man defines woman not in herself, but as relative to him; she is not regarded as an autonomous being. . . . She is defined and differentiated with reference to man and not he with reference to her; she is the incidental, the inessential as opposed to the essential. He is the subject, he is the Absolute—she is the Other."[25] As such, it is very rarely that there has existed a reciprocal relation between the sexes. Levi-Strauss points out that even the "reciprocal bond basic to marriage is not set up between men and women, but between men and men by means of women, who are only the principal occasion for it."[26]

Woman is thus the inessential, the absolute Other, without reciprocity. Every creation myth has expressed this—among others the legend of Genesis. The unilateral form of the sexual myths is a manifestation of the same idea. Elaborating on the subject, Simone de Beauvoir says:

> We sometimes say 'the sex' to designate woman; she is the flesh, its delights and dangers. The truth that for

> woman man is sex and carnality has never been proclaimed because there is no one to proclaim it. Representation of the world, like the world itself, is the work of man; they describe it from their own point of view, which they confuse with absolute truth. . . . Man seeks in woman the Other as Nature and as his fellow being. But we know what ambivalent feelings Nature inspires in man. He exploits her, but she crushes him, he is born of her and dies in her; she is the source of his being and the realm that he subjugates to his will; Nature is a vein of gross materialism in which the soul is imprisoned, and she is the supreme reality; she is contingence and Idea, the finite and the whole; she is what opposes the Spirit, and the Spirit itself. Now ally, now enemy, she appears as the dark chaos from whence life wells up, as this life itself, and as the overyonder towards which life tends. Woman sums up nature as Mother, Wife and Idea; these forms 'now mingle and now conflict,' and each of them wears a double visage.[27]

Because woman is the Other, man feminizes the ideal he sets before him. Literature down the ages bears testimony to this fact. Woman is the divine grace leading Christian towards God, she is Beatrice guiding Dante in the beyond and Laura summoning Petrarch to the lofty summits of poetry. This is one of the major archetypal patterns that Maud Bodkin delineates, and at the end of her study hypothesizes that it may be possible to find an "imaginative representation of man, related to the distinctive inner life of a woman in the same manner as an image of woman appearing in poetry shows relation to the emotional life of man."[28] Unable to find any example in classical poetry she turns to fiction by women writers and analyzes Virginia Woolf's *Orlando* and Emily Bronte's *Wuthering Heights* in the context of this theme.

To a certain extent, Bodkin's hypothesis that it may be possible to find an "imaginative representation of man related to the distinctive inner life of a woman," is borne out by Edith Wharton, Willa Cather and Ellen Glasgow, novelists whom she does not discuss. However, there is an important modification—the imaginative representation of their ideal image of man is never actualized in their fiction. Rather, the ideal is suggested through the negative portraits of the male protagonists, who are weak characters, unable to transcend the limitations imposed upon them by a convention-bound society. For example, although strongly attracted to the independent young heroines of the novels for those very qualities that make them "different," these men are yet unable to overcome a stereotyped view of women when necessary. These heroes are juxtaposed against strong female protagonists who are either trying to break out of the conventional and mythical image of woman, or have already done so. They are women who are struggling to be neither man's peer nor his master, but are rather seeking to exist as independent entities. In their relationship with men they therefore expect the latter to accept them as such. There is thus a dichotomy between what the heroines expect the male counterparts to be and what they are in reality. The female protagonists look for an ideal figure to whom they could turn for support or personal fulfillment, but each one of them is disillusioned. Some of them carve out their destiny in spite of, and in defiance of the conventional expectations of the male protagonists, while others succumb to the social pressures. Yet each one of them emerges heroic in the context of the novel concerned. As a result of the above stated dichotomy, in none of these novels do we find a fulfilling, satisfactory and viable man-woman relationship.

For a long time Edith Wharton was regarded as a lesser Henry James, Ellen Glasgow as a social historian of the South, and Willa Cather as merely an elegist of the pioneering West. Earlier critics (who were generally male) did not fail to comment on the absence in the works of these writers of male characters of heroic proportions and consequently of successful man-woman relationships. Further, they generally viewed this aspect of these novelists as a major drawback, a serious limitation of their art. Feminist critics concerned to describe a literary tradition of their own provided the impetus to look carefully at women writers. What was discovered was that writers like Wharton, Cather and Glasgow can no longer be viewed as anomalies but must be seen as major artists. Feminist critical studies played an important role in establishing the fact that these writers wrote from a distinctively female perspective of experience and in their works focussed on the roles and destinies of women. While explicating the feminist bias of these novelists, feminist critics mostly focussed on the female protagonists in these novels. For example, Elizabeth Ammons in her study of Wharton notes: "Typical women in her view—no matter how privileged, non-conformist, or assertive . . . —were not free to control their own lives, and that conviction became the foundation of her argument with American optimism for more than twenty years. . . . Her governing themes arise from the recurrent situation of a heroine perceiving an enormous and cruel lack of it between her personal expectations of life and the social reality. Where there is rebellion it almost always meets with failure."[29] The subject of Carol Wershoven's book-length study of Wharton is the "female intruder in the novels of Edith Wharton" who, according to the author, serves "as both critic of society and the carrier of positive values."[30] Linda M. Wagner's recent study of Glasgow from a feminist perspective is concerned with showing the development of Glasgow to the point where she could create female characters who were complex, whole, independent and fully human.[31] Sharon O'Brien in her essay entitled "Mothers, Daughters, and the 'Art Necessity': Willa Cather and the Creative Process," unites textual, cultural and psychological analysis to examine Cather's struggle to combine seemingly contradictory identities of "woman" and "artist," to analyse her relationship with her mother and the other women whom she loved; and considers Cather's major fiction in the light of these issues.[32] Susan J. Rosowski's essay "Willa Cather's Women" sees Cather's women as embodying "themes concerning female experience."[33] Josephine Donovan's book *After the Fall* examines the Demeter-Persephone myth in the fiction of Wharton, Cather and Glasgow.[34]

When these critics do discuss the male protagonists it is only to delineate their negative characteristics. The question as to why these three novelists consistently created male characters who were weak, unheroic and unable to live up to the expectations of the female characters has neither been asked nor answered. In this study I propose to analyze the male protagonists in selected novels of Edith Wharton, Ellen Glasgow and Willa Cather, in the context of man-woman relationships.

I shall try to show that through the negative portraits of the male characters these writers were suggesting their ideal image of man. Thus, in the works of these writers it is possible to find an imaginative representation of man related to the distinctive inner life of a woman. Far from being a weakness or a drawback, the depiction of their weak and ineffectual male characters is intentional. Further, it is this aspect of their work that is expressive of their distinctive "female sensibility," their different and unique perspective of experience and life as a whole. Their male protagonists become vehicles of their scathing attack on the patriarchal society and its institutions which would limit woman to the role of a wife and mother, and view her as an object to be possessed and subdued. Viewed from this angle, the male characters, though inefficacious, are nevertheless real and authentic. Moreover, once it is agreed that it was the conscious aim of these novelists to create negative male protagonists, our evaluation of these writers as artists would also change. Thus, it would no longer be possible to accuse them of being unable to create fully rounded male characters. Writing from a distinctively female experience of the world, their perception and hence their rendering of reality is bound to differ from that of their male predecessors and contemporaries. Their incapacity of earlier (predominantly male) critics and readers to properly interpret and appreciate these texts was, in large part, due to their ignorance of women's values or conceptions of the world. This led them to write off as trivial what they could not understand. But a re-examination of these writers in the light of the insights provided by recent developments in feminist literary criticism has revealed hitherto unexplored and hidden meanings and aspects of their works. One such unexplored aspect of these novelists is the portrayal of negative male protagonists in their fiction. By positing the thesis that through their unheroic male characters, these writers were suggesting their ideal image of man, I hope to offer a new interpretation which would lead to an enhanced understanding of the works of these novelists, of them as artists, and of their vision of life and the human condition.

A few words about why it was decided to study only ten novels may be in order here. As each of the three novelists included in this study wrote a large number of novels, a discussion of all the novels in a project of this type would have made the task unmanageable, and also have given rise to superficiality and diffusion. Therefore, for a sharper focus it was felt necessary not to consider all the works but to concentrate on a select few. The choice of the few has not been random but based on certain considerations such as: they must be representative of the writers' works on the whole, and of their treatment of the male protagonists and the man-woman relationships in particular. The novels which best illustrated the theme also happened to be the ones that are by and large, the acknowledged masterpieces of these novelists. Ten novels were felt to be optimal in terms of maintaining a sharp focus, as well as providing a persuasive and convincing argument. Four of these novels are by Edith Wharton and three each by Ellen Glasgow and Willa Cather.

While analyzing these writers' depiction of the male protagonists and the man-woman relationship, their treatment of plot and characterization has been examined closely and in detail, in each of the ten novels selected for study. Due attention has also been paid to other aspects such as the use of irony, the narrative technique and points of view, and the rationale of authorial intrusions.

In the next chapter, I will examine four novels by Edith Wharton. Three of them, *The House of Mirth, The Reef* and *The Age of Innocence* are generally considered to be among her masterpieces. *The Fruit of the Tree*, though often regarded as an artistic failure, has been included because of its relevance to the theme that I am explicating. While analyzing the depiction of the male characters, I have also examined Wharton's attitude towards such issues as the prevailing double standards of sexual morality, society's false expectations regarding women and the consequences of the economic dependence of women.

The third chapter is devoted to a discussion of Ellen Glasgow's fiction. Beginning with *Barren Ground* which marks the onset of her most creative phase, one in which she achieved her greatest artistic success, I go on to examine *The Romantic Comedians* and *The Sheltered Life*. These two novels are her well-known tragi-comedies of manners. Glasgow's portrayal of the male protagonists and man-woman relationship is the main focus of the chapter. However, certain related issues have also been discussed. For example, the patriarchal male's belief that he has a right to polygamous happiness which is a consequence of the prevalent double standards of sexual morality, and the society's failure to provide opportunities for women to develop.

The fourth chapter examines three novels by Willa Cather: *The Song of the Lark, My Antonia* and *A Lost Lady*. All the three novels belong to Cather's early period. Since her later fiction gives rise to issues which are outside the scope of this study, I have confined myself to her earlier writings. Analyzing Cather's male protagonists in the context of man-woman relationship is the major concern of this chapter. An attempt has been made to account for certain controversial issues arising out of Cather's highly unconventional mode of life and the almost total absence of dramatic relationships between men and women in her fiction.

Finally, "Conclusion" sums up the major findings of the study, links the three novelists together, and attempts to establish their relevance to the present times.

How men perceive women and what their concept of an ideal male figure is, has been depicted in literature down the ages. Edith Wharton, Ellen Glasgow and Willa Cather were among the first American novelists to express women's perceptions of men and their concept of an ideal male figure. That their ideal image is never actualized in their fiction is because, living in the society in which they did, they could not envisage the existence of such a figure. They were pioneers in the field, and their work has significant bearing on our understanding of not only the socio-cultural milieu, but of the psyche of women as well. Women's hitherto unexpressed desires, their unfulfilled expectations, and their dissatisfaction with the existing social, cultural and economic conditions are given admirable expression in their novels. Insofar as each one of them hints at the parameters upon which a viable man-woman relationship can be based, they are not only critics of their society but visionaries as well.

NOTES

1. Southey to Charlotte Bronte, March 1837. Quoted in Sandra M. Gilbert and Susan Gubar, *The Madwoman in the Attic: The Woman Writer and the Nineteenth Century Literary Imagination* (New Haven and London: Yale University Press, 1979), p. 8.
2. Elaine Showalter, *A Literature of their Own: British Women Novelists from Bronte to Lessing* (New Jersey: Princeton University Press, 1977), p. 11.
3. G.H. Lewes, "The Lady Novelists," cited in Elaine Showalter, *A Literature of their Own*, p. 3.
4. Virginia Woolf, *A Room of One's Own* (1929; rpt. London: Grafton Books, 1985), p. 74.
5. *Ibid.*, p. 71.
6. Patricia Meyer Spacks, *The Female Imagination* (New York: Alfred A. Knopf, 1975), p. 3.
7. Spacks, pp. 4-5.
8. *Ibid.*, p. 7.
9. *Ibid.*, p. 35.
10. Annette Kolodny, "Some Notes on Defining a 'Feminist Literary Criticism,'" *Critical Inquiry*, 2, No. 1 (1975), 76.
11. *Ibid.*
12. *Ibid.*, pp. 84-85.
13. Vivian Gornick, "Toward a Definition of the Female Sensibility," in *Essays in Feminism* (New York: Harper and Row, 1978), p. 112.

14. Gilbert and Gubar, p. 78.
15. *Ibid.*, p. 73.
16. *Ibid.*, p. 84.
17. Annis Pratt, *Archetypal Patterns in Women's Fiction* (Bloomington: Indiana University Press, 1981), p. 6.
18. Janet Todd, "Introduction," in Janet Todd, ed., *Women and Literature* (new series), special number on "Gender and Literary Voice" (New York, London: Holmes and Meier Publishers, 1980), p. 1.
19. Joyce Carol Oates, "Is there a Female Voice? Joyce Carol Oates Replies," in Janet Todd, ed., *Women and Literature*, p. 10.
20. Elizabeth Abel, "Introduction," in Elizabeth Abel, ed., *Writing and Sexual Difference* (Chicago: University of Chicago Press, 1982), p. 1.
21. Gerda Lerner, "The Challenge of Women's History," *The Majority Finds Its Past* (New York, 1981), p. 32.
22. Elaine Showalter, "Feminist Criticism in the Wilderness," in Elizabeth Abel, ed., *Writing and Sexual Difference*, p. 34.
23. Aristotle, "Politics," in Richard McKeon, ed., *The Basic Works of Aristotle* (New York: Random House, 1941), p. 1132.
24. Quoted in Simone de Beauvoir, *The Second Sex* (1949; rpt. Penguin Books, 1984), p. 16.
25. *Ibid.*, p. 16.
26. Claude Levi-Strauss, *The Elementary Structures of Kinship* quoted in Simone de Beauvoir, *The Second Sex*, p. 103.
27. Simone de Beauvoir, pp. 175-76.
28. Maud Bodkin, *Archetypal Patterns in Poetry* (1934; rpt. London: Oxford University Press, 1965), p. 299.
29. Elizabeth Ammons, *Edith Wharton's Argument with America* (Athens, Georgia: University of Georgia Press, 1980), pp. 3-5.
30. Carol Wershoven, *The Female Intruder in the Novels of Edith Wharton* (London: Associated University Presses, 1982), p. 17.
31. See Linda M. Wagner's *Ellen Glasgow: Beyond Convention* (Austin: University of Texas Press, 1982).
32. Sharon O'Brien, "Mothers, Daughters, and the 'Art Necessity': Willa Cather and the Creative Process," in Fritz Fleischmann, ed. *American Novelists Revisited: Essays in Feminist Criticism* (Boston, Massachusetts: G.K. Hall, 1982), p. 267.
33. Susan J. Rosowski, "Willa Cather's Women," *Studies in Ameri-*

can Fiction 9 (1981), p. 261.

34. See Josephine Donovan, *After the Fall: The Demeter-Perspephone Myth in Wharton, Cather, and Glasgow* (University Park and London: The Pennsylvania State University Press, 1989).

The Negative Hero: Edith Wharton's Male Protagonist

Aristocratic, conscious of her New York elite status, yet rebellious Edith Wharton grew up in the 1870s and 1880s in a society which not only discouraged intellectual pursuits in a woman but regarded them as somewhat deviant. A woman with a propensity for writing caused enough embarrassment to her family for them to want to guard it as a shameful secret never to be divulged. A woman's single-minded aim in life was supposed to be to make a suitable marriage and anyone who deviated from the path and tried to assert her independence intellectually or otherwise was frowned upon.

As a child, little Edith was a sore trial for her mother. Lucretia Jones did not know what to make of a child who preferred "making up" to playing with other children and reading to any other activity. Lack of understanding and encouragement proved to be a serious handicap in Wharton's growth as an artist. The following incident which she never forgot and later recorded in her memoirs *A Backward Glance*, is an example. At the age of twelve she wrote her first short story which began: "'Oh, how do you do, Mrs. Brown?' said Mrs. Tomkins. 'If only I had known you were going to call I should have tidied up the drawing-room.' Shyly she took it to her mother who returned it to her with the chilling observation that 'drawing rooms are always tidy.'"[1] Edith was so stricken by her mother's criticism that she abandoned fiction writing for three years and instead took to writing poetry. Time and again in her novels Wharton lashes out at the society that would stifle a woman writer, and whose ideal is the infantile woman as against one who is mature and independent. In fact, her youthful experiences as a writer struggling for recognition in a society averse to granting it to female artists influenced her themes to a great extent.

Often accused of being nothing more than a pioneer of interior decoration, "unconsciously shut in behind plate glass, where butlers serve formal dinners, and white shoulders go up at the mere suggestion of everyday gingham,"[2] she has been much underrated. Regarded as one concerning herself only with the "nice moral issues" of the privileged set, having nothing to do with the rise of the masses or the Union demand for a higher wage,[3] she is denied her rightful position as one of the pioneers of feminism in American literature. Although she was not among the activists who campaigned for social or legal reforms that might enhance the authority of women and although she certainly joined no women's club, she was profoundly affected by the Woman's Movement, and with *The House of Mirth*, a best seller in 1905, she became one of its most unlikely yet important and independent thinkers. Wharton's feminist bias is apparent in her portrayal of the male protagonists who are also the vehicles of her scathing attack on the existing socio-cultural milieu. The heroes of the novels included in this study do have qualities which attract strong and independent women to them, but they lack the strength of character and the moral temerity to overcome the social pressures and conventional views of women. The discrepancy between what the heroines expect their male counterparts to be and what they are in reality, and the ensuing conflict, is the concern of this chapter.

Blake Nevius was one of the first critics to point to the "lurking feminism" in Edith Wharton's novels which he said can be detected in her implied criticism of the double standard of sexual morality and "in the appearance in so many of her stories of the emotionally low-charged, over-scrupulous male protagonist."[4]

That the male protagonists in Edith Wharton's novels are weak has been noted by many. Significant among them is Irving Howe who comments upon their "notorious vanity and faithlessness," their "weak imagination" and "laziness of spirit that keeps them from a true grasp of suffering." On the basis of this, he finds in Edith Wharton's novels "a suppressed feminine bitterness, a profound impatience with the claims of the ruling sex."[5] It is, perhaps, Edmund Wilson who goes to the heart of the matter when he points out "the typical masculine figure in Edith Wharton's fiction is a man set apart from his neighbours by education, intellect, and feeling, but lacking the force or the courage either to impose himself or get away. . . . In Edith Wharton's novels these men are usually captured and dominated by women of conventional morals and middle-class ideals; when an exceptional woman comes along who is thirsting for something different or better, the man is unable to give it to her."[6]

Both Irving Howe and Edmund Wilson impute this phenomenon to a "feminine animus." Undoubtedly Wharton's male characters are the vehicle of her feminism through whom she provides a critique of the existing socio-cultural conditions. But, on probing further it becomes apparent that through the negative portraits of her male protagonists and their inability to fulfill the expectations of the heroines, the "exceptional women," Wharton implies the fictional representation of her ideal image of man.

I

The arena of Edith Wharton's fiction is the forefront of social life. In *The House of Mirth* it is New York society which she knew intimately and also knew it to be a mere veneer of hypocritical concepts. The problem was how to extract from such a subject the "typical human significance" which is the "story-teller's reason for telling one story rather than another." The answer was that "a frivolous society can acquire dramatic significance only through what its frivolity destroys."[7] In Wharton's novel, it destroys Lily Bart, the sensitive and vital heroine. The chief instrument of her destruction is Lawrence Selden, whose inconsistencies and vacillations are subtly unfolded in the course of the novel. With great insight

Wharton delineates the relationship between the two. The theme is slowly and subtly developed and reaches full flower in her later novels. Coolidge aptly says, "It [*The House of Mirth*] had found its author an amateur. It left her a professional."[8]

Lawrence Selden is, as his creator herself admitted, "a negative hero." A lawyer by profession, Selden is a bachelor who has consciously kept himself away from permanent ties. Although not brilliant or exceptional in any way, he appeals to Lily Bart because "he had preserved a certain social detachment, a happy air of viewing the show objectively, of having points of contact outside the great gilt cage in which they were all huddled for the mob to gape at."[9] Selden's distinction was that he had never forgotten the way out of the "gilt cage." What Lily fails to perceive is that this air of detachment is a form of escapism and that in reality Selden has internalized many values of the society he professes to disdain. He is not only the victim of his environment but at times "the unthinking mouthpiece of the worst of society's prejudices."[10]

Having grown up in an atmosphere where restricted means were felt only as a check on aimless profusion, and "abstinence was combined with elegance in a way exemplified by Mrs. Selden's knack of wearing her old velvet as if it were new," he has inherited "the stoic's carelessness of material things, combined with the Epicurean's pleasure in them." (152) Selden has thus imbibed a moral finickiness that is totally divorced from reality. He believes that life fully led must satisfy both his detachment from the worldly aspect and the indulgence of his keenest sensitivities. The fact that these two appetites might be mutually contradictory is a problem that Selden has no capacity to confront. Living in the society in which he does, it is not surprising that Selden projects these ambivalences into his notion of femininity. "Life shorn of either feeling appeared to him a diminished thing; and nowhere was the blending of the two ingredients so essential as in the character of a pretty woman." (152) He does not want to marry a girl who is merely "nice" (as he tells his cousin

Gerty Farrish), and Lily unadorned would certainly fail to sustain his interest. He luxuriates in Lily's decorative quality which he would have her retain, but abhors the material world that sustains it. She is merely a connoisseur's delight for him—an object to be placed on the mantle-piece and admired, not to be clasped close to the heart and cherished. Throughout the story Selden moves towards Lily from behind an armour of emotional self-protection, always afraid to give over to the commanding impulse, always defending himself against the very involvement he most desires for himself. In a perceptive analysis of Selden's character, Cynthia Wolff remarks: "There is first the self-indulgence of his appreciation of her, then the startled guilty awareness of the monetary implications of even such indulgence as this; then disapproval . . . and finally the longing to see such beauty allied in some indefinable way with the lofty virtue that his nature craves."[11] She considers his entire attitude towards Lily as one of moral-aesthetic ambiguity. Only in Lily's revivification of Reynold's portrait "Mrs. Llyod," is Selden's demand for a moral-aesthetic being fully satisfied. These ambiguities in Selden's character make him reluctant to permit serious emotional ties and he tries to evade the responsibility by finding Lily deficient.

At the beginning of the novel, Lily is twenty-nine, young, beautiful and still single. Eleven long years she has been in the public eye during which younger and plainer girls have been married by the dozen, and Lily an acclaimed beauty, is still Miss Bart. Why? It is a question that intrigues many of her well-wishers but only one, Carrie Fisher, comes anywhere near the truth when she tries to explain Lily's conduct to Selden:

> That's Lily all over, you know: she works like a slave preparing the ground and sowing her seed; but the day she ought to be reaping her harvest she oversleeps herself or goes off on a picnic. . . . Sometimes . . . I think it's because at heart, she despises the things she's trying for. And it's the difficulty of deciding that makes her such an interesting study. (189)

Lily Bart is a woman who has been trained from childhood to work for one thing: to use her beauty as a tool to gain social acceptance and the financial security that an approved marriage will bring. From the first page of the novel she is hard at work seemingly using the skills of her trade—charm, sex appeal, solicitude—to entertain and give pleasure to other people. She is adept at all the social arts, which consist of dressing well, receiving and making visits, being a helpful and engaging houseguest, and playing bridge. Thus, on the surface she perfectly embodies society's ideal of the female as decorative, subservient and submissive. But only on the surface. In reality she has merely learned to repress and camouflage her own impulses and ambitions. As Elizabeth Ammons points out, "Even though she acquits herself of the social arts in which she has been so carefully bred, she transgresses other moral and social regulations with which society expects compliance."[12] For example, she visits Selden alone in his apartment, borrows money from Ned Van Alstyne,[13] and does not hesitate to take a job as a private secretary to the nouveauriche Mrs. Hatch when the need arises. Her behaviour is non-conformist as are her real ambitions. She has "fits of angry rebellion against fate when she longed to drop out of the race and make an independent life for herself" (39). Her true aspiration is imaged in the seal on her stationery, with its flying ship and the motto "Beyond." She wants to escape, to shape her own destiny.

Lily's misfortune is that she has been trained for no trade and she is aware of this. Her dilemma arises from the fact that on the one hand she desires an independent existence, does not want to be any man's possession, and on the other, there are the social pressures working on her, forcing her into just the kind of "practical" and "advantageous" marriage that she dreads so much. Nothing expresses her innate desire for independence and her deep discontent with her own situation so well as her spontaneous cry on entering Selden's flat: "How delicious to have a place like this all to one's self! What a miserable thing it is to be a woman." (7)

Realizing that she cannot escape marriage she yet hopes to

be able to retain her independence and individuality within marriage. But that is not possible in the kind of cold-blooded, utilitarian proposal that for example, Rosedale makes to her (which is after all the accepted thing in her society). She is attracted to Selden because of his seeming unconventionality which she feels might enable him to accept her as an individual with an identity of her own. Selden's intellectual accomplishments constitute an added appeal, as Lily is an intelligent, well-read young woman who prides herself on the fact that she always carries an Omar Khayyam in her travelling bag. She turns to him because among all her male acquaintances he is the only one who comes anywhere near her ideal. So she "longed to be to him something more than a piece of sentient prettiness, a passing diversion to his eye and brain" (95). In the drama of Lily's life, Selden is the one person who could have helped her, saved her from destruction. But the ambiguities in his character that have already been pointed out, do not allow him to do so. He is the one friend who is near enough to affect her, yet keeps himself away from the vicissitudes of her life. Selden knows as well as Lily that if she is to create a life of finer values, it can be only with his help. Yet he fails to give her the support, the loving faith she needs. At every stage in Lily's downfall he is present. A close analysis of the important encounters between the two would help to make the point clear.

The novel begins with a picture seen through Selden's eyes and it is important that the reader differentiates, as Wharton does through the use of irony, between Selden's point of view and the reality of situations. The opening encounter between Lily and Selden establishes the terms of their relationship. Lily is presented only as Selden sees her, and he is shown to have the lingering, appraising mind of the experienced collector and connoisseur. He reacts to the decorative and sensuous aspect of her personality, remarking the chiaroscuro effect of "her vivid head reiieved against the dull tints of the crowd," and notes the details of her clothing and "the purity of tint, that she was beginning to lose after eleven years of late hours and indefatigable dancing" (4). As they walk up Madison Avenue the inspection continues, with Selden "taking luxurious pleasures in her nearness" (5). Lily puzzles Selden because he cannot place her either fully within or without the "herd of her sex" and so he is forced to think about her. His assessment of Lily during this encounter deals almost entirely with externals and at every point he is willing to accept the appearance for reality. Thus while it is true that many people have "been sacrificed" to "produce" Lily, he does not realize that the principal sacrifice has been Lily herself. When Lily tries to move beyond the superficialities of their relationship and attempts frankness, he responds first with a nervous evasion into inconsequential flirtation, and then takes refuge in expressing the society's point of view: "Isn't marriage your vocation? Isn't it what you're all brought up for"? (9) Thence, their conversation turns into an inventory of Lily's chances for marriage, and Selden continues with his "appreciation" of Lily now that he has placed her at a safe emotional distance. Commenting on the scene C.G. Wolff says, "Selden is thoroughly encapsulated in his own preoccupations, needs and prejudices."[14] He is reluctant to enter into any serious emotional ties and the judgmental quality of his manner precludes sympathetic response. On the other hand Lily is (as is apparent even in this first exchange) ready to meet him on some common emotional ground.

Their second encounter, which takes place at Judy Trenor's house party at Bellomont, reveals the moralistically righteous side of Selden's personality. All Lily's practical intentions disappear when Selden arrives at Bellomont. During the quiet afternoon they spend together in the midst of nature's beauty, Lily realizes that for the first time in her life she is really in love with a man. Selden draws her on to talk about her plans and her failure to find success. Turning on her "worldliness," he attacks her ambitions and predicts a miserable future for her if she continues with her present goals. He then outlines his own image of success which consists in maintaining a kind of "republic of the spirit." It is a vision that she can aspire to, as it is a republic that offers freedom "from everything—from money, from poverty, from ease and anxiety, from all the material accidents" (68). Lily is attracted to this Utopian vision, a "country one has to find the way to one's self" as Selden says in response to her expression of regret that there had been no one to tell her about it. However, she cannot help questioning the genuine workability of Selden's system as she realizes that he is offering her a standard he himself does not live by. Advising her that very few of the rich can ever enter the "republic of the spirit" Selden is himself exposed by Lily's wry observation that he seemed to spend a lot of time in the element he disapproved of. The comment only elicits the evasion that he is an "amphibious" creature. Selden's very presence at Bellomont, an environment he is teaching Lily to despise, indicates that Lily's criticism is a valid one.

His attitude of sustained condemnation wears away at Lily's confidence. She cries out "You despise my ambitions—you think them unworthy of me." (71) And again, "Why do you do this to me? . . . Why do you make the things I have chosen seem hateful to me, if you have nothing to give me instead?" (72). Lily's works move Selden to a declaration, and her answering tears almost, but not entirely, break his stance of ironic detachment.

At this point the lovers seem united in some higher sphere: "The soft isolation of the falling day enveloped them: they seemed lifted into a finer air. All the exquisite influences of the hour trembled in their veins, and drew them to each other as the loosened leaves were drawn to the earth" (73). However, the communion cannot be sustained for long. In order to be worthy of Selden's "collection," Lily must not waver in her disdain for the "things" of this world: as little as a fleeting hesitation will betray sufficient flaw. In the quiet of the sensitive scene between Lily and Selden, the shrill horn of a motor car strikes the note of discord, breaking the dreamlike quality of the communion. Lily falters, remembering the excuse she has made to other guests, and Selden's somewhat softened manner changes into one of harshness and contempt.

The moment of "perfect harmony" is revived for a short time during the Bry's *tableaux vivants*. Having dispensed with a sumptuous setting and costume, Lily has become the "real" Lily. To Selden it seemed "as though her beauty . . . had held out suppliant hands to him from the world in which he and she had once met for a moment, and where he felt an ever mastering longing to be with her again" (135). Once again he is moved to a declaration of his love. However, his inability to have faith in Lily again destroys the moment of "perfect union." Seeing her emerge from Gus Trener's house late in the evening he puts the worst possible construction on it. Although Lily is, ironically, not guilty of the transgression he imputes to her, his capacity for understanding is so slight that he is incapable of knowing her true situation. His own affair with Bertha Dorset scarcely justifies the chaste horror he manifests at the possibility that Lily's conduct has been less than absolutely perfect. It is, in fact, evidence of Selden subscribing to the prevailing double standards of sexual morality.

Hereafter she evokes little more than ironic, detached disapproval from him. Instead of offering her any genuine help, he merely stands aloof, stern, contemptuous and censorious, as for example, during his visit to her at Mrs. Hatch's apartment. Her sorrows to him are trivial, artificial, "even her weeping was an art." She saves face in Italy by an adoption of "the Grand Manner"; and Selden characteristically accepts this fiction. His egotism pictures her as definitely divided from him by the "crudeness of a choice which seemed to deny the very difference he felt in her—the choice in which she was content to rest: in the stupid costliness of the food and the showy dullness of the talk, in the freedom of speech which never arrived at wit and the freedom of act which never made for romance." (216)

Their last encounter takes place, like the first one, in Selden's apartment. It is here that Lily rises to her one act of genuine heroism. She burns Bertha Dorset's letters to Selden (and it is significant that Selden never does know that they were in Lily's possession and that she has nearly sacrificed herself to preserve his reputation) which she could have used as a key to her social rehabilitation. It is her love for Selden which prompts her to this act and surely C.G. Wolff is mistaken in supposing that Lily's capacity for love has atrophied,[15] and so is Louis Auchincloss when he says that "Lily Bart's love for Lawrence Selden is the one hollow note of *The House of Mirth*.[16] It is ironical that she performs this noble act in Selden's presence when he is embarrassed by her misery and openness. Broken down by the misfortunes and vicissitudes of her life, Lily can only exclaim piteously, "I needed the help of your belief in me" (308) and is willing to take the entire blame for the failure of their relationship solely on herself. However, the reader who can be objective, knows what a major role Seldon has played.

The next morning, when he rushes to Lily, having finally "found the word he means to say to her," it is too late and he is confronted by the lifeless corpse. While going through her few possessions, even at this juncture he suffers loss of faith. Discovering a letter to Trenor, he feels himself "flung back on all the ugly uncertainties from which he thought he had cast loose forever." (327) Not until he realizes that Lily had carefully saved a note he had written her after the tableaux does Selden link the "real" Lily he had perceived that day to the Lily "still there on the bed, close to him, yet invisible and inaccessible" and face his own complicity in her destruction. He is forced to acknowledge "the cowardice which had driven him from her at the very moment of attainment." (328)

Keeping in mind Selden's capacity for self-deception, he is not likely to salvage much from the ruin of his life, but whatever he does will be due to his involvement with Lily Bart which has taught him some unpleasant truths about himself.

Lawrence Selden is undoubtedly a "negative hero." Weak, vacillating and inconsistent, he is largely responsible for Lily Bart's tragic end. He espouses an ideal of success, "the republic of the spirit," a standard by which he himself does not live. To begin with, the moral-aesthetic ambiguities in his character and his escapist attitude do not allow him to enter into a serious emotional relationship with Lily. When he is finally able to overcome the ambiguities in his attitude to Lily and is ready to make a commitment, his double standards of sexual morality prove to be a stumbling block. He turns away from Lily and is almost happy that he is "safe" from any involvement. Lily who is trying to break through the traditional roles imposed by society upon women, needs the support and understanding of someone like Selden. Selden's inability to transcend the conventional views of society and provide the necessary support to Lily results in the break up of a relationship which could have been successful and satisfactory.

II

In her next novel *The Fruit of the Tree*, Wharton claimed to have satisfied those of her readers who had complained about the "negative" hero in *The House of Mirth* by trying to create a strong and dynamic character in the person of John Amherst. Unlike Selden, he is a man of passion and action with a strong commitment to his work and a zeal for social and industrial reform. High-principled, warm and virile, he is yet utterly tradition-bound. It is in his attitude to women and his expectations from them that he is revealed to be an essentially weak and conventional man, who is also lacking in imagination.

Critics point out that *The Fruit of the Tree* attempts so much that it does not do justice to its separate strands, and the book as a whole does not hang together.[17] This long intricately plotted novel deals primarily with two problems: social reform and euthanasia, and at the centre of each problem is John Amherst. It is he who links the various parts of the novel, and if Wharton gives a comparatively sloppy, vague picture of factory life in the novel, it is because she is only vaguely interested in industrial reform. Mainly she is interested in the relationship between John Amherst, the would-be reformer and the two women he gets involved with—Bessy Westmore and Justine Brent. In this novel, as in the two subsequent ones *The Reef* and *The Age of Innocence* Wharton introduces two women characters—a conventional tradition-bound woman (an example of the existing stereotpye) who acts as a foil to the strong, independent, rebellious woman—the embodiment of Wharton's deep-rooted convictions and values.

Amherst, the assistant manager of the Westmore Mills, prides himself on his independence from narrow intellectual and moral views. His enlightened ideas about industrial and social reform fly in the face of accepted tradition and the maxims he seems to value most, contend: "We perish because we follow other men's examples. . . . Socrates used to call the opinions of the many by the name of Lamiae—bugbears to frighten children."[18] Yet when Justine administers the overdose of morphine to the maimed and suffering Bessy, Amherst is repelled—he is unable to act on the principles he advocates and to overcome traditional notions about women which do not allow for independent thought and action in them. The son of a mechanical genius and a "lady," he disappoints his mother by joining the working classes instead of taking up a profession like his grandfather, Judge Warne. However, at heart he is, like his mother, quite a snob. He keenly feels the lack of family fortunes, not only because lack of money renders him unable to initiate his desired reforms, but also because it places him in a position of subordination. His snobbish attitude comes to the fore in his initial encounter with Bessy Westmore. Although he works for Bessy and depends on her for his livelihood, he does not see himself as her inferior; rather he desires that "Mrs. Westmore should not regard him as less of her own class than his connections and his upbringing entitled him to be thought." (68)

Until Amherst met Bessy, he had never thought much about women. "He had vaguely regarded them as meant to people that hazy domain of feeling designed to offer the busy man an escape from thought" (559). His interaction with Bessy does nothing to alter this idea as she is beautiful and dependent, the product of society's false expectations of women. As Mrs. Ansell, Wharton's spokeswoman says, she is "one of the most harrowing victims of the plan of bringing up our girls in the double bondage of expediency and unreality, corrupting their bodies with sentiment and leaving them to reconcile the two as best they can, or lose their souls in the attempt." (281) In a perceptive analysis of Bessy's character

Elizabeth Ammons contends that Bessy is "the adorable blonde from 'The Valley of Childish Things' brought to life ten years later in a realistic drama. . . . She is the precious child-woman preferred by men and therefore valued by the culture over her adventurous adult sister, in this case Justine."[19] The novel bears out Ammons's contention, as Amherst at the beginning as well as at the end of the novel prefers Bessy, the "child-woman" to Justine, her "adult sister."

It is Bessy's beauty, "which was like a blinding light turned on eyes subdued to obscurity," (42) which first attracts Amherst to her. Her soft, pliant nature and her ability to make Amherst believe that she entered into all his thoughts, add to the appeal. Although he realizes that her curiosity is too purely personal and emotional to lead to any larger understanding of the question, he regards this concentration on the personal issue to be the "compensating grace of her sex" (119). Apart from this, Bessy fascinates Amherst for many reasons, some of which he conceals from himself. He has a genuine desire to transform Bessy, the frivolous socialite, into a compassionate reformer, "to see the angel of pity stir the depths of those unfathomable eyes, when they rested, perhaps for the first time, on suffering that it was in their power to smile away as they had smiled away his own distrust." (47) In his desire to remake Bessy, Amherst's egotism is revealed.

Moreover, Bessy's money is an added attraction as it would give him the power he craves to do good and restore him to what he feels is his proper station in life.

The marriage proves to be disastrous for both the partners. Amherst, who "had always conveniently supposed that the poet's line summed up the good woman's rule of ethics: 'He for God only, she for God in him'" (179), expects Bessy to conform to his ideas and accept his ideals as her own. In other words, he expects her not only to give him entire control of her fortune and allow him to bring about the desired changes at the Westmore Mills, but to share his zeal for industrial reform as well. Bessy has, however, married Amherst, not out of love of good deeds, but for love of the man himself. When she discovers that her love is not reciprocated, she retaliates by denying Amherst the total control of finances that he had expected to be his. Further, she thwarts his objectives by spending freely and frivolously on her personal pleasures. However, her behaviour does not stem from purely selfish motives. Underneath all her pliability and superficiality there is a certain amount of stubbornness, and an instinctive realization that if she played the passive role expected of her and surrendered control of the mills, she would totally cease to exist for Amherst.

Justine Brent is one of Wharton's warmest characterizations, and as has been pointed out by many, the author put more of herself into this character than in any other. Having experienced the loss of the family fortunes as a child, she has been forced to earn her own living, with the result that she has developed an individuality and a strength of character not at all in consonance with the accepted notions of femininity, though she is at the same time one of Wharton's first heroines to be aware of, and to frankly acknowledge her own needs as a woman. Justine excels at her profession because it provides an outlet for her energetic nature which, unlike Lily Bart's, has not been suppressed. She thrives on physical and mental activity and the challenge of responsibility, both of which her profession disciplines and channels into useful service. She has no desire to turn herself into a social ornament or a domestic decoration. She combines culture and refinement with self-sufficiency and social activism. Being economically independent as well, she has no desire to marry merely for wealth and a position in society. Even Amherst realizes that she could never be drawn to the kind of man who "needed fine clothes and luxury to point him to the charm of sex" (450). She was certainly not one who attached "much importance to the upholstery of life. . . . No, the man who won her would be of a different type, have other inducements to offer" (450). Those "other inducements" being, besides mental and intellectual companionship, an implicit acceptance of her as an individual with the ability to think and act independently. In Amherst she sees a glimpse of this ideal. His nonconformism in the professional sphere, and his general indifference to the norms and appearances of society give rise to this belief in Justine, a belief which is destined to be shattered.

The novel opens with an encounter between Justine and Amherst. In this very first meeting a bond is established between the two. Each appreciates and understands the other's desire to alleviate the pain and suffering of the downtrodden with which their respective professions bring them into close contact. When she next meets Amherst, he is married to Bessy Westmore who happens to be Justine's friend from schooldays. At Bessy's request, Justine takes up residence with her as nurse and friend. Although she loves the luxury of the world Bessy inhabits, the people in it, she feels she "missed the poetry of their situation" (221). She feels trapped in the shallow social world of Lynbrook and longs for "a life in which high chances of doing should be mated with finer forms of enjoying." (223)

At the time of Bessy's fatal riding accident, her marriage has completely broken down and Amherst is away in South America. As she lingers on in terrible pain with little hope that she will ever recover she indicates to Justine that she wants to die. Justine remembers her conversation with Amherst regarding the maimed mill-worker.

> "I know what I should do if I could get anywhere near Dillon—give him an overdose of morphine, and let the widow collect his life-insurance, and make a fresh start.
>
> She looked at him curiously. "Should you, I wonder?"
>
> "If I saw the suffering as you see it, . . . In your work, don't you ever feel tempted to set a poor devil free?"
>
> She mused. "One might . . . but perhaps the professional instinct to save would always come first."
>
> "To save—what? When all the good of life is gone?" (15)

At the same time, she comes upon Amherst's inscription on the flyleaf of one of his books, "Socrates used to call the opinion of the many by the name of Lamiae-bugbears to frighten children" (429). Because she thinks it is what Amherst would want, and because she can no longer bear to watch Bessy in agony, Justine gives her a fatal overdose of morphine. Her own conscience on this matter is absolutely clear, and so convinced is she that Amherst would consider her action justified that she does not feel it incumbent on her to reveal the fact to him.

Two years later Justine accepts Amherst's proposal, as he seems to be a man of liberal sentiments and advanced views. In addition, he respects Justine and welcomes her aid as a fellow reformer. To Justine, marriage to Amherst seems the fulfillment of her desire to do good in a beautiful setting. Together they could design and institute changes that would make life safer and more pleasant for the mill-hands and their families. Her desire for meaningful work at first blends with Amherst's philanthropy: "their duties had the rare quality of constituting, precisely, the deepest, finest bond between them" (472). For a while Justine finds married life as fulfilling as she had hoped it would be. She and her husband plan and carry out reforms, discussing them at his office and at home in the Westmore mansion. Above all, the couple enjoys an uninhibited mental and sexual compatibility that fulfills their open and passionate natures. But the marriage soon founders as Amherst learns about the euthanasia.

Wharton makes it clear that Justine should undoubtedly have given Bessy the lethal overdose of morphine. The tragedy centres in her husband's inability to accept that action. Justine while reviewing her action in the light of her husband's attitude to it is still convinced that her "motive had been normal, sane and justifiable. Her fault lay in having dared to rise above conventional restrictions, her mistake in believing that her husband could rise with her" (525). Justine, while surveying his character, perceives that Amherst, like many men of emancipated thought, had remained subject to the old conventions of feeling. Having never given much thought to women he "had always been content to deal with them in the accepted currency of sentiment" (525). Although there had existed a deep intellectual accord between the two of them, and they were truly wedded in mind as well as in heart, she realizes that until the issue of euthanasia came up between them, "there had not arisen in their lives one of those searching questions which call into play emotions rooted far below reason and judgment in the dark primal depths of inherited feeling. It is easy to judge impersonal problems intellectually, turning on them the full light of acquired knowledge" (526). What pains Justine most is that Amherst had not understood her, had in fact judged her as the world might judge her.

Amherst's reaction to Justine's act of euthanasia proves his essential conventionality. As Carol Wershoven remarks, "Amherst's inability to stand by and support Justine is the most negative aspect of his character and belies his radical posings."[20] The stumbling block for Amherst is not the fact that it was Bessy, his first wife, who was the recipient of the euthanasia. He knows that she was hopelessly estranged from him at the time of her death. He never doubts that Justine, as the nurse on the case, helped her friend die out of compassion, with no thought of personal benefit. What makes it difficult for Amherst to accept Justine's action is the fact of her having performed it on her own initiative, out of her own sense of moral autonomy, and not having felt bound to seek his approval after the action. Undoubtedly his relationship with Justine has led him to "the blissful discovery that women can think as well as feel," a discovery that has made him discard his former first wife, who was the recipient of the euthanasia. He knows that she was hopelessly estranged from him at the time of her death. He never doubts that Justine, as the nurse on the case, helped her friend die out of compassion, with no thought of personal benefit. What makes it difficult for Amherst to accept Justine's action is the fact of her having performed it on her own initiative, out of her own sense of moral autonomy, and not having felt bound to seek his approval after the action. Undoubtedly his relationship with Justine has led him to "the blissful discovery that women can think as well as feel," a discovery that has made him discard his former summary conception of woman as "a bundle of inconsequent impulses, and admit her at a stroke to full mental equality with her lord" (560). Yet it is clear that what Wharton sardonically calls "this act of manumission" does not grant woman real mental or moral independence from "her lord." Justine's unforgivable offence is to have kept her own counsel. "His mind could assent—at least in the abstract—to the reasonableness of her act; but he was still unable to understand her having concealed it from him" (560). That she has not concealed her act, but simply never felt it her duty to bring it up, Amherst can never conceive. Analyzing Amherst's relationship with Justine, Elizabeth Ammons comments: "Despite his liberal views, he remains utterly convention-bound in his inability to understand that Justine does not consider herself morally accountable to him."[21]

Thenceforth, nothing of their former intimacy, which was based on a free camaraderie of mind, remains. Amherst makes it clear to Justine that he no longer wants to work with her on an equal basis at the mills, and Justine has no choice but to accept the changed relationship. The conclusion of the novel gets to the root of the issue. Fourteen months later Justine attends the dedication of the Westmore Mill gymnasium. Unaware of the fact that Bessy, out of spite for his having spent her money on industrial and social reforms, actually had the gymnasium designed for her personal use, Amherst in his eloquent speech erroneously credits it to his dead first wife. As Amherst eulogizes a Bessy who never existed, "a wave of anger swept over Justine at this last derisive stroke of fate. It was grotesque and pitiable that a man like Amherst should create out of his regrets a being who had never existed, and then ascribe to her feelings and actions of which the real woman had again and again proved herself incapable!" (628)

Faced with a woman too independent for his tastes, Amherst retreats, like other Wharton males, for example Newland Archer of *The Age of Innocence*, from the living woman, and turns for solace to an ideal: to a romantic, old-fashioned image of Bessy. The wilful, selfish Bessy whom Amherst almost hated is now transformed into what Margaret McDowell describes as "a suppliant saint, a person whom he could love"[22] because he would be able to dominate her.

John Amherst is in some ways a more positive character than Lawrence Selden. He certainly has some likable qualities—strength of character and determination, a dynamic personality, and enlightened views on social and industrial reform. However, despite his advanced opinions on social issues, his views regarding women are extremely conventional. He adheres to the traditional belief that women are in some sense inferior to men and should therefore remain subservient. Even after he has experienced the joys of being wedded to a woman like Justine who can "think as well as feel" and with whom he shares an uninhibited mental and physical compatibility, he is unable to accept the fact that Justine can act on her own initiative and not feel answerable to him. His inability to accept Justine as an equal, one who is capable of independent thought and action, mars a relationship that could have proved to be fulfilling to both partners. Once again Wharton makes her point clear— no viable and satisfactory relationship is possible between a woman who is inherently capable, intelligent and independent, and a man who is essentially conventional.

III

In 1912, Wharton published *The Reef* commonly described as being her most Jamesian novel, one which had a "psychological Racinian unity, intensity and gracility."[23] As a vehicle for her mature style *The Reef* is comparable to *Ethan Frome* and *The Age of Innocence*, and is a tribute to her versatility in adapting style to subject. With great skill and dexterity, Wharton reveals the working of the consciousness of two of the three main characters—George Darrow and Anna Leath. The characterization of Sophy Viner, although refracted through the consciousness of Darrow and Anna, is striking in its definiteness and individuality of outline.

There has been a certain amount of controversy as to what is Wharton's attitude towards Darrow and Sophy. For example,

Blake Nevius is of the opinion that a "strong personal bias is evident in the lenient treatment of Darrow's case as opposed to that of Sophy" and that "Sophy Viner's future is foreshadowed in the vulgar outlines of her sister's career."[24] However, as I will show, Wharton neither condones Darrow's action nor does she mean to portray Sophy as a negative character. On the other hand, Wharton makes it clear that the tragedy in the novel is perpetrated by Darrow's double standards of sexual morality and it is Sophy who emerges as the heroine of the piece.

Darrow is the least attractive of the Wharton males included in this study. Like Selden he is a dilettante, desultorily pursuing the diplomatic profession. Having imbibed the values of the society in which he lives, he has conveniently categorized women as those that are pronouncedly "ladies" and those that are not. He was certainly grateful to both for "ministering to the more complex masculine nature,[25] having always assumed that they had been evolved, if not designed, to that end. Nevertheless, he had instinctively kept the two groups apart in his mind, and had avoided that intermediate society (Bohemian) which attempts to conciliate both theories of life. Sophy Viner intrigues and interests him because she does not fall into either of the two categories principally because they are ways of construing the feminine nature that make it entirely ancillary to masculine needs. Women, even women who are not entirely "nice" will react but not act—so Darrow has always held. Yet Sophy has had experience, and "her experience had made her free without hardness and self-assured without assertiveness" (27). A "New Woman," very much like Justine Brent, but without the latter's professional skills, Sophy is a foil to the conventional Anna Leath. In this novel, as in *The Fruit of the Tree* before and *The Age of Innocence* after, Wharton uses the device of double female protagonists. Darrow's character is delineated through his relationship with the two women. Both of them have an ideal image of man in their mind and in differing ways look to Darrow to satisfy this ideal. Anna, brought up in the typical old New York way, and schooled in reticence, evasion, and a kind of artificial serenity that have denied her any sexuality, looks to him for emotional and sexual awakening. Sophy, on the other hand, sees in Darrow a composite image of a man of the world, whose experiences in life have (so she thinks) liberated him from the narrow outlook and prejudices of the society in which they live. The expectations of both the women are belied and Darrow is to a large extent responsible for wrecking Sophy's life and happiness.

Anna Summers Leath is the embodiment of Darrow's ideal of womanhood (which incidentally coincides with that of the society in which he lives). A perfect example of ladylike repression she had, in her early youth, at times perceived that other girls, leading outwardly the same life as herself, were "yet possessed of some vital secret that escaped her" (87). Having grown up in the well-regulated world where the unusual was regarded as immoral or ill-bred, and people with emotions were not visited, she now perceived that there had always hung a veil between herself and life. Love, she told herself, would one day release her from this spell of unreality. She had been sure that some day, "she would find the magic bridge between West fifty-fifth Street and life" (88). It's in the person of young Darrow that she first caught a glimpse of this "magic bridge." His extraordinary intelligence and his tall, fair, easy presence greatly added to his charms. However, the romance was nipped in the bud by the unfortunate accident of Darrow engaging in a mild flirtation with Kitty Mayne, one of those young women who, unlike Anna, were acquainted with "the arts of life." Years later, after an unfulfilling marriage and subsequent widowhood, Anna is still in quest of this "magic bridge." It is ironical that once again she should look to Darrow, a man who is not only as conventional as herself, but who is also, as Margaret McDowell says, "trapped in the conventional pattern of thinking that categorizes women as either 'fallen' or 'pure.'"[26] While Anna looks to George Darrow for a sexual and emotional awakening and for entry into the world outside of Givre, Darrow, who has already enjoyed the company of "bad" women, is looking to Anna for the consolations of a "good" one. Her very narrowness and her limitations appeal to Darrow. His imagination is struck by "the quality of reticence in her beauty. She suggested a fine portrait kept down to a few tones, or a Greek vase on which the play of light is the only pattern" (127). It is clear that Darrow sees in Anna an exquisite aesthetic object that he would like to keep unsullied from contact with real life.[27] He certainly dreams of putting "warmth in her veins and light in her eyes," of in fact, making her "a woman through and through." Yet, he is convinced that this sexual initiation will serve only to make Anna more exclusively his, even more "like a picture so hung that it can be seen only at a certain angle known to no one but its possessor. The thought flattered his sense of possessorship." (130) Further, she was the kind of woman with whom "one would like to be seen in public." In short, for Darrow, Anna is just a possession in whom he can take pride. She is the limited "good" man, and Givre a "pure sequestered shrine." (146) Here Wharton attacks not only Darrow but also the culture that suppresses women and encourages them to believe that love and marriage will some day release them into "reality."

In his relationship with Sophy Viner, Darrow for the first time comes in contact with a woman who is neither conventionally "good" nor "bad." She is, as she herself says "awfully modern," and does not really "believe in marriage" but is "all for self-development and the chance to live one's life." (62) Her wish never to marry and her skepticism about the institution in general are analogous to Lily Bart's fear of marriage in *The House of Mirth*. Having had to fend for herself from an early age, she is, as Darrow soon perceives, "distinguished from the daughters of wealth by her avowed acquaintance with the real business of living," yet he does not feel that reality has corrupted her; rather "her experience had made her free without hardness and self-assured without assertiveness" (27). Possessed of a clarity of thinking which enables her to see that her greatest handicap is lack of any professional skill, she has a very sensible plan when the novel opens. She wants to become an actress. So far financial need has always kept her from trying her luck, but now she hopes to earn enough money as a governess in Paris to pay for acting lessons. Her plan fails and she is forced to take up a position at Givre which is too far away from Paris. Her decision to accept Anna's stepson, Owen Leath's proposal of marriage is the logical outcome of her situation as she does not want to remain a governess all her life. Sophy faces the dilemma of Lily Bart and all women who were not independently wealthy. Lack of economic security often forced these independent young women into a marriage not of their choice. Sophy almost capitulates to the inevitable. In the end, however, she (once again like Lily Bart) changes her mind and bravely decides not to contract herself to a man she does not love.

When Darrow meets Sophy she is adrift, without a job; and he is also at a loose end having received a cryptic and curt telegram from Anna putting him off from joining her at Givre. Intrigued by her frank and easy manner, he tries to label Sophy, just as Archer attempts to classify Ellen: "She might be any one of a dozen definable types, or she might—more disconcertingly to her companion and more perilously to herself—be a shifting and uncrystallized mixture of them all." (60). Unable to classify her, he is however, soon moved to compare her with Anna and to the latter's disadvantage. He begins to wonder whether the "sheltered" girl's up-bringing might not unfit her for all subsequent contact with life. In spite of her marriage and motherhood, and the passage of fourteen years, Anna Leath, with all her reticences and evasions, was no nearer to it. Even her freshness now appeared to Darrow like the unnatural whiteness of flowers forced in the dark. The outcome of such reflections is that Darrow finds himself having an affair with Sophy. He initiates the affair for several reasons, almost all of which he hides from himself. His motives include anger at Anna for betraying his ideal of her, wounded vanity ("She became of absorbing interest to him as an escape from himself and an object about which his thwarted activities could cluster" (56), and a genuine attraction to Sophy. Besides, Sophy serves as a convenient salve to Darrow's bruised ego. It does not take him long to see that she has led a very repressed life and is exceedingly lonely. "The girl had been dying for some one to talk to, some one before whom she could unfold and shake out to the light her poor little shut-away emotions." (39)

Given her stifled and repressed past, it is but natural that Sophy reacts to even the smallest kindness with an overwhelming gratitude and appreciation. With an almost cruel detachment Darrow observes her happiness in Paris: "Her delight in the fresh air, in the freedom, light and sparkle of the morning, gave him a sudden insight into her stifled past; nor was it indifferent to him to perceive how much his presence evidently added to her enjoyment" (39). Taking advantage of her starved and lonely youth, Darrow is sporadically affectionate towards Sophy, knowing fully well how she is likely to respond to his affections.

Thus, in order to bolster his own image of himself and to lash out against his damaged image of Anna, Darrow turns to Sophy. Apart from these two motives, Darrow becomes sexually involved with Sophy for a much less complex reason. He genuinely likes her. Her naturalness which could ease a "situation of constraint" is a refreshing change from the studied poise of Anna Leath. During his interaction with her, he sees how easy it is to explain things to her. Either she would accept his suggestion, or she would not. She would certainly "waste no time in protestations and objections," nor make any "vain sacrifice to the idols of conformity." (37)

The affair comes to an end when Darrow receives the long-awaited letter from Anna. But when it arrives Darrow throws it, unopened, into the fire. This action, as Geoffrey Walton remarks, suggests that the affair with Sophy "means more to Darrow than he later admits to himself."[28]

The truth about Sophy and Darrow comes to light in a series of complex and subtle scenes by what Anna calls "the force of its irresistible pressure." Wharton uses each stage in these painful revelations to further explore the hidden recesses of the personalities of the three main characters.

When Darrow learns about Sophy's engagement to Owen Leath, his reaction is ignoble and hypocritical. It is a blend of self-interest, class-consciousness and an unquestioning acceptance of the double standard of sexual morality. He is unable to overcome the doubts commonly held about the woman who tries to rise above her past. According to him their affair makes Sophy unfit to marry Owen and he desperately wants to prevent her from doing so. However, it never occurs to him that the same yardstick may be applied to himself as well; that his conduct is just as condemnable. Darrow is too much a product of the society that looks upon extra-marital affairs as damning to a woman but only mildly reprehensible in a man. Certainly Lawson is mistaken when he says that Wharton's treatment of the double standard in the novel is "disappointing" and that she "went so far as to offer a rationalized and inhumane defense of the standard."[29] What Wharton does is to lash out against this in the novel.

Having decided that Sophy should not be allowed to taint the sacred atmosphere of Givre, Darrow quietly goes about trying to effect her removal from that place. He tries to bribe, coax and Cajole Sophy into breaking her engagement. When none of these methods succeed, he does not scruple to use the one argument which he knows will have a profound effect on her. He tells her that "you'll be wretched if you marry a man you're not in love with." (206) Sophy, out of love for Darrow, acts with such generosity that she puts him to shame. She not only breaks off her engagement to Owen, but makes it clear that she intends to sever all links with the family.

When Darrow thinks of the affair in Paris, it is with a sense of exasperation and self-contempt, as in that episode he "had fallen below his own standard of sentimental loyalty," (152) and if he thought of Sophy it was mainly as the chance instrument of his lapse. It is only an unpleasant memory which has cast an unsavory shadow on his estimate of himself. On the contrary, for Sophy, the days with Darrow are a cherished memory in spite of the fact that she no longer has any illusions about his love for her. She now knows and openly admits that Darrow never loved her: "I wonder what your feeling for me was? It seems queer that I've never really known—I suppose we don't know much about that kind of feeling. Is it like taking a drink when you're thirsty? . . . I used to feel as if all of me was in the palm of your hand." (259) The episode, then, is important to Sophy not because it was a fairy-tale romance, but rather because it was the only chance she ever had, and possibly will have, for giving her love, and for receiving the kindness and understanding so lacking in her life. In her brief relationship with Darrow, she had for the only time in her life felt that she was being accepted and liked on her own merits as an individual. Even though she learns later that Darrow is not the man she thought him to be, that he also subscribes to the values and prejudices of his society, she continues to love him and has no regrets because "He was good to me—no one ever was so good." (283)

The last scene of the novel has been interpreted by many critics as Wharton's indictment of Sophy. Further, they have regarded Anna as being justified in classifying Sophy as a sexual adventuress. For example, Blake Nevius says, "By the time Anna Leath's visit occurs, Sophy has set off for India with Mrs. Murrett, a notorious London hostess from whose service she had originally fled. Blood will tell. Water will seek its own level."[30] Margaret McDowell comments: "Sophy's sister, a singer, is undoubtedly a courtesan, and she foreshadows for Anna what Sophy may with years become."[31] Lawson also reads the last scene as a denigration of Sophy which he however considers to be "cruel and gratuitous."[32]

However, these critics fail to realise that it is Anna who sees the disturbing similarities between Sophy and her sister and not Wharton. A more tenable interpretation is Geoffrey Walton's, who describes the scene as "a scathing comment on Anna. She goes to look for Sophy and finds real coarseness and vulgarity in her sister, and one is made to realize beyond any doubt the distinction of Sophy's character which has survived its environment with a simple integrity that Anna, with all her refinement cannot achieve."[33] What the scene highlights is a contrast between Anna's naivete and horror of such a situation, and Sophy's ability to transcend it.

Commenting on Sophy's character, Carol Wershoven says: "Like Ellen Olenska in *The Age of Innocence*, it is Sophy

Viner who emerges as the big 'winner' in the novel, because she has taken the risks that life in the real world involves, and because she has given—given her love without hope of reciprocation, and given up all chance of the wealthy and pleasurable life Owen offers so that Darrow can be happy. The small fears, subtle withdrawals, and timid advances of Darrow and Anna are a shadowy backdrop for Sophy's glowing act of courage."[34]

Undoubtedly, Sophy Viner is the heroine of the piece. She represents the positive values of her world.[35] She emerges as the most human of the trio in the novel, the most sensitive to other's emotions, and the most honest about her own. Although she lacks Ellen's sophistication, her culture and cool self-assurance, she is, like the latter, capable of true passion and willing to sacrifice for those she loves. Unfortunately, her sacrifice does not really benefit anybody. The only realization that dawns on Darrow is that in having an affair with Sophy en route to Givre he committed a loathsome and shameful act. It does not lead to any reassessment of his values in life. He is thus left to a life with Anna and the perpetual surveillance of a jealous and disillusioned woman.

Through the character of George Darrow, Wharton launches a scathing attack on the society that encourages the double standards of sexual morality and categorizes women into either "good" or "bad." The most contemptible of her "negative" heroes, Darrow has a few redeeming qualities. He is utterly self-centered, smug and complacent. Owing to his inability to overcome the inherited biases regarding women, he is responsible for wrecking the life and happiness of Sophy Viner. He not only enters into a relationship with Sophy when he is already engaged to Anna, but also succeeds in ruining Sophy's chances of making a career for herself as an actress. Once more Wharton reiterates her belief that a successful relationship between a weak and conventional man like Darrow and a strong "modern" and inherently independent woman like Sophy is impossible.

IV

The last of her major novels, *The Age of Innocence* is generally considered to be Wharton's masterpiece. Margaret McDowell says: "In *The Age of Innocence* she [Wharton] wrote her most consistently articulated and sophisticated novel . . . [it] reveals the writer's discipline and her creation of a form absolutely suitable for her subject."[36] Her subject, of course, remains the same. Once again she depicts a male protagonist, Newland Archer, attractive in certain ways, yet weak and vacillating insofar as he is unable to overcome the inherited prejudices and biases regarding women. His is the sole point of view in the novel, although it is one that Wharton distances herself from by irony and supplements with authorial comment.

An intelligent young man, what distinguishes him from the other males in the novel is his interest in reading on wide-ranging topics as well as in painters and artists. He is moreover, desirous of keeping up with such interests. He is the only one among the fashionable gentlemen to consort with "clever people" like Ned Winsett and "probe into things a little deeper than the average level of club and chop-house banter" (122). It is these traits that attract Ellen to him as he is the only one with whom she can interact on a level that she has been used to in European society.

However, there is another side to Archer—a much less attractive and perhaps a more dominant one. Like Selden and Darrow, he is by nature "a contemplative and a dilettante."[37] He is complacent about and delighted with his own promising but not taxing law practice, with the adoration of his widowed mother and his sister, and the love of his beautiful and unimaginative fiancee. He takes great pride in his own taste for books and his eye for pictures and is rather smugly satisfied that he has sowed his wild oats in a desultory affair with a married woman which he feels has prepared him to cope with his future wife's assumed ignorance in all matters of sex. His conventionality is apparent in the routine parting of his hair with two silver-backed brushes, the flower in his lapel, and his provincial pride at being a New Yorker, though, ironically, he considers himself to be a cosmopolitan.

In this novel, Wharton once again depicts two female characters—the fair, conventional child-woman, May Welland, and the dark, sensual, mature adult, Ellen Olenska. The novel begins with the juxtaposition of the two women and the worlds they represent. At this juncture, Archer, a somewhat pompous and self-satisfied young man, has just declared his allegiance to the conventional world by proposing marriage to May Welland. May is, as Elizabeth Ammons notes, "Wharton's rarefied version of the stereotype."[38] She is always associated with white: her virginity, mentally and emotionally, cannot be touched. She is permanently pure, and, Wharton implies, permanently juvenile. She has a fresh "boyish" quality that brings to mind the "invincible innocence" of her middle-aged mother, and suggests that May too will go through life sexually unaware and armed in innocence. Her innocence is the innocence in the title of the novel, the kind that, in Wharton's words, "seals the mind against imagination and the heart against experience." It is an innocence that does not prevent her from feigning reluctance during courtship or from being aware of the advantages of the prescribed long engagement itself; nor does it exclude a calculated shortening of that engagement, or even complicity in the hypocritical banishment of Ellen. Wharton makes it abundantly clear that innocent May is both ancient and artificial. "In spite of her athletic freedom and bright modern cheeriness, she is as old as patriarchy itself. Intently observing her at the opera, Archer realizes that she does not understand the seduction scene being played on stage, and feels "a thrill of possessorship" which constituted "pride in his own masculine initiation" mingled with "a tender reverence for her abysmal purity" (7) Like John Amherst, Archer has visions of forming and educating his innocent bride. He also has ambitious plans for the development of his fiancee into the woman he wants her to be:

> He did not in the least wish the future Mrs. Newland Archer to be a simpleton. He meant her (thanks to his

> enlightening companionship) to develop a social tact and readiness of wit enabling her to hold her own with the most popular married women of the "younger set," in which it was the recognized custom to attract masculine homage while playfully discouraging it. If he had probed to the bottom of his vanity (as he sometimes nearly did) he would have found there the wish that his wife should be as worldly-wise and as eager to please as the married lady whose charms had held his fancy through two mildly agitated years. . . . How this miracle of fire and ice was to be created, and to sustain itself in a harsh world, he had never taken the time to think out. . . . In matters intellectual and artistic Newland Archer felt himself distinctly superior of these chosen specimens of old New York gentility. . . . Singly they betrayed their inferiority; but grouped together they represented "New York," and the habit of masculine solidarity made him accept their doctrine on all issues called moral. He instinctively felt that in this respect it would be troublesome—and also rather bad form—to strike out for himself. (7-8)

The irony in this passage creates the impression of a fatuous, egotistical young man who blithely adheres to the prevailing double standards.

Although May's ignorance and innocence pander to Newland's masculine vanity, yet when he tries to imagine a comradely marriage with her, he is somewhat depressed as he perceives that it required on her part the experience, versatility and freedom of judgement which she had been carefully trained not to possess. He knows that she is never likely to surprise him with a new idea or emotion. Further, he realizes that because "of this elaborate system of mystification" to which girls are subjected, May has no depth: "she was frank, poor darling, because she had nothing to conceal, assured because she knew nothing to be on her guard against" (45-46). Yet Newland knows that untrained human nature is neither frank nor innocent. In fact it is "full of the twists and defenses of an instinctive guile. And he felt himself oppressed by this creation of factitious purity" (46) which ironically has been manufactured solely for his pleasure. This ambivalence in his attitude towards May continues throughout the novel, and it marks his relationship with Ellen as well.

Having always subscribed to the belief that there was an "abysmal distinction between the women one loved and respected and those one enjoyed—and pitied," (97) his meeting with Ellen, a woman who fits into neither of the categories, has an almost catastrophic effect on him. Were it not for the arrival of Ellen Olenska, the beautiful, disenchanted cousin of his fiancee who had fled from a titled Polish brute of a husband, Newland would have probably spent his life in a complacent, predestined way within his society. Ellen is not only a sophisticated, sexually exciting woman, she is also a highly imaginative and passionate person capable of independent thinking. Thus it is but natural that she should want to get a divorce from her husband and lead her life independently, much as a bachelor might.[39]

Archer's inability to categorise Ellen adversely affects his relationship with her. For example, he cannot understand her association with the "shoe polish queen," Mrs. Lemuel Struthers. Mrs. Struthers, a parvenu with a scandalous past who is trying to entice New York society to her Sunday evening cultural entertainments, is shunned by Archer's group, yet Ellen visits her, taking along an English duke. Instead of accepting this action as an example of the fact that true aristocrats feel secure enough to cross social boundaries, Archer is irked by Ellen's flagrant violation of the New York code.

These ambiguities in his attitude to Ellen continue throughout the novel. Whenever he feels threatened by Ellen (and her world) who has the "mysterious faculty of suggesting tragic and moving possibilities outside the daily run of experience," he runs to May the "safe" alternative: "Here was truth, here was reality, here was the life that belonged to him" (141). The very fact that he sees Ellen as being "outside the daily run of experience" makes it inevitable that he will abandon her and choose May. For to Archer marriage to Ellen is never a real possibility. Her place in his life is similar to that of his books, his intellectual friends, and his cultural interests. They are not a part of real life, but an escape from it. Thus he can only imagine her as a fantasy woman, one he could have married if circumstances had been different. In fact, Archer could make the fantasy into reality. He could break his engagement to May, but he is unable to overcome his inherited biases. Besides this, another aspect of his character comes into play, which is hinted at in the first pages of the novel: "thinking over a pleasure to come often gave him a subtler satisfaction than its realization" (4); the fantasy is better than the reality. So his avowal of love is also made in terms that imply its futility: "you are the woman I would have married if it had been possible for either of us" (169). However, as Ellen points out, it is he who has made it impossible by persuading her not to get a divorce. Archer has chosen to live by the standards of New York, and Ellen holds him to the consequences of that choice.

From Ellen, Archer not only learns about love, but her honest perceptions of the New York society prick the bubble of his complacent acceptance and open his eyes to its falseness. It is she who stirs up "old settled convictions and set[s] them drifting dangerously through his mind" (43). Under this influence he makes his first apparently revolutionary statement: "Women ought to be free—as free as we are," without realizing its full impact. That he really does not subscribe to such a notion is made clear to us by Wharton's authorial comment that Archer's statement "struck to the root of a problem that it was agreed in his world to regard as non-existent." It was inconceivable for nice women, however wronged, to claim the kind of freedom he meant, and "generous-minded men like himself were therefore—in the heat of argument—the more chivalrously ready to concede it to them" (44). That Archer does not really advocate freedom for women is made clear to us insofar as he is the person mainly instrumental in persuading Ellen not to press for a divorce. The arguments he uses to dissuade her are that she would bring great pain and misery to her family by such an action and that it was necessary that the happiness of the individual be sacrificed to the welfare of the tribe. However, Wharton makes us feel that perhaps Archer would not have been so keen upon dissuading her from her plan if she had vehemently denied that she had anything to fear from her husband's threat and that she had no illicit relationship with the man who helped her to run away from her husband. Still firmly entrenched in New York ways of thinking, he wants to hear Ellen protest her innocence before he allies himself with her in her struggle for freedom. Archer's action repudiates his earlier assertion that Ellen had every right "to make her life over" and that he was "sick of the hypocrisy that would bury alive a woman of her age if her husband prefers to live with harlots" (42). Here we see him subscribing to the double standard of sexual morality. His allegiance to this code, time and again proves to be a stumbling block in his relationship with Ellen. In fact it is largely responsible for the tragedy that occurs in this novel. The very traits in her character that attract him—her maturity and her lack of ignorance and innocence—are traits which his social conditioning has taught him to associate with women who are not "nice." Thus, even in their moments of intimacy, her past intrudes and he cannot curb such reflections as: "A woman who had run away from her husband—and reputedly with another man—was likely to have mastered the art of taking things for granted." (238). At another time, after having persuaded her to agree to a clandestine meeting he "stared after he in a turmoil of contradictory feelings. It seemed to him that he had been speaking not to the woman he loved but to another woman he was indebted to for pleasures already wearied of. . . . 'She'll come!' he said to himself, almost contemptuously." (308-309)

A prey to such contradictory feelings, it is not surprising that Newland Archer does not have the courage to throw overboard all conventional norms and marry Ellen. However, as he cannot curb his attraction for her, he selfishly suggests to her an ignominious alternative and is shocked when she asks bluntly: "Is it your idea, then, that I should live with you as your mistress—since I can't be your wife?" (312) What startles him most is that Ellen had not only used a word that women of his class evaded even when their talk flitted closest about the topic, but pronounced it as if it had a recognized place in her vocabulary.

Ellen's rejection of this offer comes as no surprise to the reader. Archer's initial sympathy had led her to believe that he understood and appreciated her and so she had begun to love him. But she is finally disillusioned and has to forego her dreams of meeting the ideal man. May's connivance has only the effect of expediting the denouement, not of changing it. Ellen Olenska leaves New York as she realizes that she cannot lead an independent life there, and sets up her own establishment in Paris. Like Amherst, Archer chooses in favor of juvenile May as against mature Ellen. His choice recalls the theme of Wharton's early parable "The Valley of Childish Things."

With Ellen's departure from his life, Archer is permanently trapped. Moreover, his choice of remaining faithful to May ironically traps her as well into an existence of dullness and emptiness. For, although Archer had once dreamed of forming and educating May, he finds after marriage, that it was less trouble to conform with the tradition and treat May exactly as all his friends treated their wives than to try to put into practice the ideas with which his "untrammeled bachelorhood had dallied." (193)

In the last chapter we see him at the age of fifty-seven, contentedly reviewing his uneventful life and having no regrets. Although he had done little in public life, he has had high things to contemplate, great things to delight in; and the friendship of one great man has been his strength and pride. He had been, in short, a "good citizen." In spite of being trapped by memory and habit, there were times when he realized that he had missed something, "the flower of life." When he thought of Ellen Olenska, "it was abstractly, serenely, as one might think of some imaginary beloved in a book or a picture: she had become the composite vision of all that he had missed." (347) Yet he would rather continue to miss out on life than dare meet Ellen again. Pathetically, he cherishes his memory of May (and Ellen) over the reality of seeing Ellen. As Elizabeth Ammons comments: "Memorializing the fair child-woman while fearing the dark adult, the once daring but basically conventional hero finally affirms his culture's preference in women."[40]

Critics like C.G. Wolff[41] and Louis O. Coxe[42] who find Archer's conforming to tradition as something admirable have apparently missed Wharton's point. She has certainly not tried to posit Archer as an ideal or as any kind of a positive figure, for she could not envisage a hero rising above the double standards and narrow confines of society. However, he is perhaps the most positive of her negative heroes. Although he fails to overcome the double standards of sexual morality and the conventional views regarding women, he does at times realize that in forsaking Ellen, he has missed something, "the flower of life." Thus, Wharton by implication indicates those positive traits which would make him the ideal man for Ellen Olenska, her female protagonist in the novel.

Wharton's male protagonists are undoubtedly weak and ineffectual beings. But they are by no means artistic failures; rather, they are real and authentic characters. Writing out of a distinctively female experience of reality, Wharton consciously created such negative characters because, given the socio-cultural milieu in which she lived, she could not conceive of them in any other terms. Nor could she envisage a successful man-woman relationship. Her male characters resemble men as she saw them around her in real life. However, insofar as she depicts her male protagonists trying to overcome the conventional views regarding women, she does by implication suggest those positive qualities which her ideal image of man would possess. Such an ideal being would be able to understand the needs and aspirations of an emancipated woman like for example, Ellen Olenska, and provide the necessary support to her in her struggle for an independent existence. This would lead to a successful man-woman relationship. Thus, although Wharton never depicts fulfilling man-woman relationships in her novels, she does suggest the foundations on which a satisfactory and viable relationship can be built.

NOTES

1. R.W.B. Lewis, *Edith Wharton: A Biography* (New York, Harper and Row, 1975), p. 30.
2. Vernon L. Parrington, "Our Literary Aristocrat," in Irving Howe, ed., *Edith Wharton: A Collection of Critical Essays, Twentieth Century Views* (Englewood Cliffs, N.J.: Prentice Hall, 1962), p. 153. Henceforth referred to as Edith Wharton, TCV.
3. Van Wyck Brooks, *The Confident Years: 1885-1915* (New York: E.P. Dutton, 1955), pp. 283-300.
4. Blake Nevius, *Edith Wharton: A Study of Her Fiction* (Berkeley: University of California Press, 1961), p. 85.
5. Irving Howe, "The Achievement of Edith Wharton," in *Edith Wharton, TCV*, p. 15.
6. Edmund Wilson, "Justice to Edith Wharton," in *Edith Wharton, TCV*, pp. 26-27.
7. Cited in R.W.B. Lewis, *Edith Wharton: A Biography*, p. 150.
8. Olivia Coolidge, *Edith Wharton* (New York: Charles Scribner's Sons, 1964), p. 82.
9. Edith Wharton, *The House of Mirth* (1905; rpt. New York: Charles Scribner's Sons, 1969), p. 54. All further references will be to this edition of the book and shall be incorporated in the text.
10. C.G. Wolff, *A Feast of Words: The Triumph of Edith Wharton* (New York: Oxford University Press, 1977), p. 111.
11. C.G. Wolff, "Lily Bart and the Beautiful Death," *American Literature*, 46 (1974), p. 28.
12. Elizabeth Ammons, *Edith Wharton's Argument with America* (Athens, Georgia: University of Georgia Press, 1980), p. 32.
13. Lily's reflections on the double standards of society that allow a married woman to live on other men, but frown upon a single woman who borrows money even from an old man, are pertinent.
14. C.G. Wolff, "Lily Bart and the Beautiful Death," p. 29
15. *Ibid.*, p. 35.
16. Louis Auchincloss, "Edith Wharton and her New York," *Edith Wharton, TCV*, p. 23.
17. Refer to R.W.B. Lewis, *Edith Wharton: A Biography*, p. 181, and C.G. Wolff, *A Feast of Words: The Triumph of Edith*

Wharton, p. 139.

18. Edith Wharton, *The Fruit of the Tree* (1907; rpt. London: Virago Press, 1984), p. 429. All subsequent references will be to this edition of the book and shall be incorporated in the text.
19. Elizabeth Ammons, *Edith Wharton's Argument with America*, p. 52.
20. Carol Wershoven, *The Female Intruder in the Novels of Edith Wharton* (London: Associated University Presses, 1982), p. 129.
21. Elizabeth Ammons, *Edith Wharton's Argument with America*, pp. 50-51.
22. Margaret McDowell, *Edith Wharton* (Boston: Twayne Publishers, 1976), p. 54.
23. Henry James, cited in R.W.B. Lewis, *Edith Wharton: A Biography*, p. 327.
24. Blake Nevius, p. 135
25. Edith Wharton, *The Reef* (1912; rpt. New York: Charles Scribners Sons, 1965), p. 26. All further references to the book will be incorporated in the text.
26. Margaret McDowell, p. 60.
27. Refer to *The House of Mirth* where Selden regards Lily Bart as a moral-aesthetic object.
28. Geoffrey Walton, *Edith Wharton: A Critical Interpretation* (Teaneck: Fairleigh Dickinson University Press, 1970), p. 65.
29. Richard H. Lawson, *Edith Wharton* (New York: Frederick Ungar Publishing Company, 1977), p. 63.
30. Blake Nevius, p. 140.
31. Margaret McDowell, p. 61.
32. Richard H. Lawson, p. 59.
33. Geoffrey Walton, p. 70.
34. Carol Wershoven, p. 104.
35. She is comparable to Ellen Olenska, the carrier of positive values in *The Age of Innocence*.
36. Margaret McDowell, p. 94.
37. Edith Wharton, *The Age of Innocence* (1920; rpt. New York: Charles Scribner's Sons, 1970), p. 346. All further references to the book will be incorporated in the text.
38. Elizabeth Ammons, "Cool Diana and the Blood-Red Muse: Edith Wharton on Innocence and Art," in Fritz Fleischmann, ed., *American Novelists Revisited: Essays in Feminist Criticism* (Boston: G.K. Hall, 1982), p. 213.

39. Refer to Lily Bart's exclamation in *The House of Mirth*, "'How delicious to have a place like this all to one's self,' What a miserable thing it is to be a woman." (7)
40. Elizabeth Ammons, *Edith Wharton's Argument with America*, p. 152.
41. C.G. Wolff, *A Feast of Words: The Triumph of Edith Wharton*, p. 333. She says: "In the end he has gained more than he has lost: he has not rejected his unique moment in history. . . . His final act affirms the coherence of his own identity, and in this assertion of 'self,' Newland achieves genuine maturity."
42. Louise O. Coxe, "What Edith Wharton Saw in Innocence," *Edith Wharton, TCV*, p. 157. Coxe goes to the extent of saying that What Newland has lost is not Ellen, but May, whom he never took pains to know or love, May who knew all along the extent and the fullness of her husband's sacrifice.

The Polygamous Male: Ellen Glasgow's Protagonist

I had grown up in the yet lingering fragrance of the old South; and I loved its imperishable charm, even while I revolted from its stranglehold on the intellect."[1] This statement points to an essential aspect of Ellen Glasgow's life and art. Although as woman and as writer she managed to exist within the cultural and literary confines of the times, she yet lived and wrote as she wanted. She was certainly the first to revolt against "the formal, the false, the affected" in the Southern literary tradition of the time.[2] What the South needed most, she once said, was "blood and irony." A realist, she looked at life around her with eyes that were neither clouded by sentiment nor veiled by romance. In her fiction, she was one of the first to strike a note of realism in Southern literature which was until then, steeped for the most part in escapism and romanticism.

However, what she revolted against most, both in life and in art, was the restrictions that the society placed upon women. In the socio-cultural milieu in which she grew up,. it was almost unimaginable for a woman to desire intellectual or professional fulfillment. Society conspired to thwart the mental development of a young girl. The education of a genteel lady comprised learning to read and write, a smattering of arithmetic, geography and history, with emphasis on deportment and fine arts. In short, she was groomed to fulfill the roles of a wife and mother. Ironically, an essential quality for being an ideal wife and mother was assumed to be a false innocence and ignorance about life.[3] The more ignorant a young girl was of the facts of life the better equipped she was considered to be able to deal with it. Over and over again, Ellen Glasgow in her novels has criticized the patriarchal society that conspires to produce this factitious purity and innocence—an unnatural state which proves to be inherently dangerous.

The lot of women, who were brought up to believe that their only aim in life was to make a suitable marriage, was not one to be envied. Glasgow gives a vivid description of the normal condition of womanhood:

> Women waiting for the first word of love from their lovers. Women waiting with all the inherited belief in the omnipotence of love, for the birth of their sons. . . . Women waiting beside the beds of the sick and dying—waiting—waiting.
>
> As a result I think it is almost impossible to overestimate the part that religion, in one form or another, has played in the lives of southern women. Nothing else could have made them accept with meekness the wing of the chicken and the double standard of morals.[4]

Early in life, Glasgow rebelled against this notion of womanhood when she decided to be a writer. Because of the hostility of her family towards her role as writer, her early work was written in secret to escape ridicule. In *A Certain Measure* she recalls: "When a bound copy of my first book reached me, I hid it under my pillow while a cousin, who had run in for breakfast, prattled beside my bed of the young men who had quarrelled over the privilege of taking her to Easter German."[5] It was not only her family that was not encouraging, but the attitude of the society in general was just as discouraging. The following incident that she cites in her memoirs *The Woman Within* is an example. When the manuscript of her first novel was completed, she took it to New York to be published. With great trepidation she approached Price Collier of the Macmillan publishing house, who took her to lunch but offered her no encouragement, rejecting the manuscript without reading it. "'The best advice I can give you,' he said with charming candor, 'is to stop writing, and go back to the South and have some babies.' And I think, though I may have heard this ripe wisdom from other men, probably from many, that he added: 'The greatest woman is not the woman who has written the finest book, but the woman who has had the finest babies.'"[6] And when the novel, *The Descendant* was published, an elderly kinsman declared it to be incredible "that a well-brought-up Southern girl should even know what a bastard is."[7]

These personal experiences played an important role in shaping her personality and gave rise to her most persistent themes as a novelist. Maxwell Geismar describes her as "a feminist with a vengeance."[8] Unlike Edith Wharton, she was a self-acknowledged feminist, a suffragist who joined the Virginia League for Woman Suffrage. Twice she marched in suffrage parades; first in London with May Sinclair, and again in New York in 1911. She believed that "suffrage for women is an inevitable fact in the social development of the race, and sentiment is as powerless to stay its coming as it is to stem the advancing tide of evolution."[9] However, even though she evinced a certain interest in women's suffrage, she was not deeply concerned with specifically feminine political goals, such as divorce, responsibility for and guardianship of children, inheritance rights, legal facilities denied to women, equal salaries, and so forth. Rather, she was more interested in the intellectual and moral emancipation of women—in women's need for mental development and a life outside the emotions. This concern is inevitably translated into her fiction. It is best depicted in the weak and satirical portraits of the male protagonists who are advocates of the patriarchal culture norms, and the fundamental incompatibility between masculine and feminine expectations regarding the "womanly woman" resulting in unsatisfactory man-woman relationships. The delineation of this theme is the concern of this chapter.

In contrast to her heroines, Glasgow's male protagonists are weak characters. Louis Auchincloss observes:

> Like Edith Wharton, she will be remembered for her women, not her men . . . in *Virginia* the weak, selfish,

> deserting male makes his appearance, and he is to stay through to the end of her fiction . . . all are faithless more from the weakness of their characters than the force of their passions. What is most appalling in Miss Glasgow's indictment is that the only ground of redemption that she can find in those of whom she regards as redeemable, . . . Miss Glasgow's heroines, . . . are devastated by her worthless men, and it is just here that her fiction is pulled most seriously out of line."[10]

Stanley Godbold in his biographical study of the fiction of Ellen Glasgow notes: "With satire and irony, with pathos and levity, she manipulated the men in her novels and in her life with the expertise of a professional artist who knew all too well the bitterness of a broken heart. Men are morally inferior to women, she decided, and deserve nothing from women but amusement and contempt. Yet men cannot escape their attraction and need for the superior female."[11] Blair Rouse writing about Glasgow's "civilized men" says: "It has been observed that many of Ellen Glasgow's women appear stronger in relation to most of the males in her novels. In other words, Miss Glasgow has been thought of as a novelist who portrayed weak or victimized or, occasionally, evil men but admirable and often very strong women."[12]

All three agree that the male protagonists are weak in relation to the female protagonists and that this is a serious drawback in Glasgow's fiction. Without looking for an adequate reason for this, they (except for Stanby Godbold who perhaps reads too much into the fact that Glasgow, in spite of being engaged thrice, never got married) dismiss it as an inability on her part to create strong, fully-rounded male characters. I would like to suggest that Glasgow created weak, convention bound male characters because she could not conceive of them in any other terms. Given the socio-cultural milieu in which she grew and lived, she was aware of the fact that the ideal male figure she had in mind, one who would be able to accept an intellectually and morally emancipated woman, did not exist. And so, through these negative portraits of men,

Glasgow is perhaps suggesting her ideal image of man.

Thus, I would concur with Emily Clark's assessment of Glasgow's handling of men: "With Jane Austen she shares, an attitude to men notable among women writers. In regard to them she is unillusioned rather than disillusioned, for her view of them is clear-eyed and quite unjaundiced. It is without bitterness, without malice, without prejudice and without glamour."[13]

With the writing of *Barren Ground* (which she described as "a vehicle of liberation") Glasgow embarked on the most creative phase of a long literary life. In fact her reputation rests principally on this novel, and two of the tragi-comedies of manners, *The Romantic Comedians* and *The Sheltered Life*, which are part of a trilogy. These novels immediately followed *Barren Ground.* During the writing of *Barren Ground* her mind had been steeped in the sense of tragic life, but soon after she finished it, "the comic spirit, always restless when it is confined, began struggling against the bars of its cage."[14] The result was a series of novels written in a vein of humour, but humour tinged with irony and satire. Glasgow makes very effective use of these devices to convey her thoughts.

I

Barren Ground remained Glasgow's favourite novel, for in it she learned to break away from the conventions of the historical novel or the novel of manners, and write the story in which the mind of a character is the theatre for the drama. As she said in her preface to the novel: "Dorinda was free, while the theme was still undeveloped, to grow, to change, to work out her own destiny."[15] Glasgow's enthusiasm for the novel never diminished. "It is the best book I have written"; "the one of my books I like best"; "putting my whole heart in a book in which I *believe.*"[16] Even if it is not her best novel (and critical opinion on this point varies) it is significant in that in it she created her most memorable and yet controversial character, Dorinda Oakley. It is also the first novel in which she uses a single point of view—the mind of Dorinda "and nothing enters the scope of the novel which might not have fallen within range of her experiences or imagination. All that the author, or reader, know of the situation is that it has meant to Dorinda, either through her consciousness, or through the impressions which persons or objects have left upon her."[17]

The story may be about Dorinda Oakley but the person who has a very significant impact upon her life is Jason Greylock, the male protagonist of the novel. Jason is an extremely weak man; he is, in fact, almost contemptible in his weakness. Although he is a doctor by profession, we soon learn that the decision to study medicine was forced on him by his father, an alcoholic old man of loose morals but an iron will. All his failures in life he attributes to the fact that as a child his spirit was broken by his father and that the force of circumstances had been too much for him. The decision to return to Pedlar's Mill and take up his father's failing practice, a bitter pill which he has had to swallow, has also been thrust on him as he is too soft-hearted to ignore his ailing parent's wish. He even pledges to stay with his father as long as the latter is alive—a promise that ultimately dooms him. He feels that he has always been balked or bullied out of having what he wanted in life, a feeling that has grown out of an incident in childhood. He tells Dorinda how he had once gone out with his mother to gather dewberries, and just as he had found the finest brier and was about to pick it, "a moccasin snake struck out at my hand. I got a fit, hysterics or something, and ever since then the sight of a snake has made me physically sick. Worse than that, whenever I reach out for anything I particularly want, I have a jumping of the nerves just as if I expected a snake to strike."[18]

In his first encounter with Dorinda he appears in a rather favourable light. He is an attractive young man with a charming, boyish smile. His gestures, like his personality, appear to be firm and energetic. However, even at this juncture the author hints at the inherent weakness of his character. While replying to Dorinda's query as to why he had returned to Pedlar's Mill so soon, a "haunting pathos" could be detected in his eyes; "the pathos of heroic weakness confronting insurmountable obstacles." (25) That his impulses are basically good is borne out by the fact that he has an altruistic desire to "enlighten the natives," to instill a few modern ideas into their heads as they do not know the first principles of farming. But the poor response his efforts evoke completely defeats him and he gives up all his ideas of reforming the farmers. Once again his lack of determination is revealed as, instead of persevering in his efforts, he admits that he is easily discouraged and takes recourse to railing against fate. Born lazy and lacking initiative he needs the contact with other minds to prod him into energy. He knows that it is a critical time for him and he must get away from Pedlar's Mill soon, or else he is doomed. He is also aware that he has already started feeling as if the broomsedge were growing over him and strangling the little energy he ever had. Yet he allows the broomsedge to claim him. He is attracted to Dorinda precisely because she is strong. He frankly tells her: "You put something in me that I need. I don't know what it is—fibre, I suppose, the courage of living." (88)

Dorinda embodies the author's personal ideal of success, something that Glasgow reiterated more than once. A character fully realized in the fiction, she has been criticized as being abnormal because some readers are not willing to accept the premises of success established by the author. Glasgow considered Dorinda Oakley to be a satisfied, well functioning human being. Yet to her biographer, E. Stanley Godbold, Dorinda was "a mechanized human being totally drained of humanity," a character who could have been created "only by an embittered and cynical woman."[19] And, according to Wayne Lesser, "she is an ambitious woman who openly expresses her contempt for weakness, who neither gives nor can receive deep affection, . . most audiences would regard Dorinda as an eccentric character."[20]

At the beginning of the novel Dorinda is like any other young girl of her time in that she believes that marriage is the only goal for a woman and falling in love would in some mysterious way open the gates to an enchanted existence. Her involvement with Jason and the subsequent desire to marry him is as much a product of socio-cultural conditioning as of sexual attraction and an unfulfilled romantic temperament. However, even at the age of twenty she is fundamentally different from those around her as she is searching, questing, with a zest for life which makes her look "as if she were running toward life." (3) She not only wants to flee from the humdrum poverty of Pedlar's Mill, she also resents the near-slavery of having to be a wife in such poverty. "Her nature, starved for emotional realities, and nourished on the gossamer substance of literature, found its only escape in the fabrication of dreams." (10) Although she had never defined the sensation in words, there had been moments when it seemed to her that her inner life was "merely a hidden field in the landscape, neglected . . . yet with a smothered fire, like the wild grass running through it. At twenty her imagination was enkindled by the ardour that makes a woman fall in love with a religion or an idea." (10) Dorinda hungered for "adventure, happiness, even unhappiness, if it were only different." (11)

The advent of Jason Greylock on the scene, who has an aura of the unknown lingering about him, provides her with a suitable object on which to fix her emotions. In the person of this attractive young man who with his physical attributes combines intelligence, amiability and filial devotion, she finds the romance and adventure for which her soul had craved. However, even during courtship she has some misgivings and she realizes that "only to a woman are love and happiness interchangeable terms." (84) This feeling prompts her to question her mother about love and marriage. The exchange between them on the subject is a bleak deflation of any notion of "romance." Mrs. Oakley does not mince words: "Grandfather used to say that when a woman got ready to fall in love the man didn't matter, because she could drape her feeling over a scarecrow and pretend he was handsome. . . . The way I've worked it out is that with most women, when it seems pure foolishness, it ain't really that. It's just the struggle to get away from things as they are." (81) To emphasize the truth of Mrs. Oakley's comment, Glasgow underlines it by showing Dorinda's surprise and chagrin: "To get away from things as they really are. Was this all there was in her feeling for Jason; the struggle to escape from the endless captivity of things as they are? In the bleak dawn of reason her dreams withered like flowers that are blighted by frost." (81) It is important that the stunting of Dorinda's romantic dreams occurs here, long before she knows she has been betrayed. In a sense, Dorinda's real betrayal is more than Jason's abandonment; it is as ageless as history, and stems from the failure on the part of parents as well as society to create lives of promise for their daughters. When Dorinda questions her mother further, Mrs. Oakley speaks directly to the point of self-actualization—feminine independence: "'Marriage is the Lord's own institution and I s'pose it's a good thing as far as it goes. Only," she added wisely, "it ain't ever going as far as most women try to make it. You'll be all right married, daughter, if you just make up your mind that whatever happens, you ain't going to let any man spoil your life.'" (81) On hearing her mother's words, Dorinda emphatically decides that she would never allow any man to spoil her life. And so, even in moments of close intimacy with Jason "she could not sink the whole of herself into emotion; something was left over, and this something watched as a spectator." (89)

Jason betrays Dorinda not because he is a villain or a scoundrel but because he is too weak to overcome external pressures. He certainly loves Dorinda enough to want to jilt Geneva Ellgood whom he had courted the year before in New York. But, when her brothers come after him he, as his father puts it, "turned white-livered again. They took him off and married him while he was still shaking from fright." (117) When Dorinda first learns of his perfidy, she is shocked into numbness: "she could not think, or, if she thought, her thoughts were beyond her consciousness, skimming like shallows over a frozen lake. Only the surface of her could feel, only her skin, and this felt as if it would never be warm again." (123) After what seemed an age she began to come back to existence. "And while life fought its way into her, something else went out of her for ever—youth, hope, love—

and the going was agony." (123) She feels trapped, as if life "had caught her," more so because she is carrying Jason's child. In a state of desperation she tries to kill Jason, but the gun misfires. True to his character, he tries to absolve himself of any guilt and elaborates on his own suffering in a vain attempt to gain Dorinda's sympathy.

> So you know. But you can't know all. Not what I have been through. Not what I've suffered. Nobody could. It is hell. I tell you I've been through hell since I left you. I never wanted to do it. You are the one I care for. I never wanted to marry her. It was something I couldn't help. They brought pressure on me that I couldn't bear. They made me do it. I was engaged to her before I came back. It was in New York last summer. She showed me she liked me and it seemed a good thing. Then I met you. I never meant to do it. But I did it. You will never understand. I told you that I funked things. I have ever since I can remember. It's the way my mother funked things with my father. Well, I'm like that, so you oughtn't to blame me so much. God knows I'd help it if I could. I never meant to throw you over. It was their fault. They oughtn't to have brought that pressure to bear on me. . . . He went on endlessly, overcome by the facile volubility of a weak nature. (129)

His double standards are apparent when he suggests to Dorinda that she continue her relationship with him even though he is married. Rather confidently he asks her "you won't give me up, will you?" (130) However, his words have no effect on her and she knows that nothing that he can ever say in the future would make any difference to her. "In that instant, with a piercing flash of insight, she saw him as he was, false, vain, contemptible, a coward in bone and marrow. He had wronged her; he had betrayed her; he had trampled her pride in the dust; and he had done these things not from brutality, but from weakness" (130)

This encounter effectively kills all her love for Jason.

Though she is aware that there are women who could love even when they hated, she knows herself to be different. "The vein of iron in her nature would never bend, would never break, would never completely melt in any furnace." (133) Realizing that Jason is a coward, she wonders how she could have loved him. Looking back on her previous encounter with him and despising him most bitterly, she yet "thought not of the wrong he had done her, not of his treachery and his betrayal of her love, but of the way he had looked in the moonlight, with his chalk-white face, his jerking muscles, and his arm waving with the gestures of an evangelist." (133) But though her mind had broken away from him, her body was still held a prisoner as so slight a thing as the memory of his smile had the power to awaken the "familiar vibrations." It is a long time before she can free her body as well from his influence.

After his betrayal of Dorinda, Jason goes downhill quite rapidly. Leading a cat and dog life with his wife, he takes to drink and starts losing all his practice. Aware of his treachery towards Dorinda, the villagers are not willing to trust a man who has been unable to honour his commitments. This adds to his speedy downfall. In short, the broomsedge grows over him as he had at one time feared. However, he makes no attempt to prevent the decline, all too ready to lay the blame on fate and others. Two years later when he meets Dorinda, he is still harping on the same theme: "If you'd given me a chance, I'd have done anything you wanted. . . . If only you knew what I've suffered. . . . I have started drinking like father." (236-37) When Dorinda tells him that he means nothing to her, he is shocked as he is unable "to believe that a woman's love can perish while his own still survives." (237)

Years later, when his passion for Dorinda has died he can dispassionately commend her on her success and on the fact that she made her life in spite of him. However, even now he is tempted to give facile explanations for his conduct:

> It was too much, I suppose, to expect you to understand how I failed. I never ran after women. That wasn't my

> weakness. I never wanted to do any of the things I did. . . . All the same I wish you could understand I was not the kind of man to do the things I did. I was a different sort of fellow entirely. But what I was never seemed to withstand the pull of what I was not. Of course, you will never see that. You'll go on thinking I was born rotten inside. Perhaps you're right. I don't know. I can't work it out. (367)

Realizing that others were not to blame he is yet unwilling to take the blame on himself and attributes everything to fate. "It was the way things turned out. . . . If father had died sooner, it might have been different. But everything happened too late. The broomsedge grew over me before I could get away." (362)

His final degradation comes about when, after being forced to sell his farm Five Oaks and living in abject poverty for some time, he is taken to the poor-house, from which he is rescued by Dorinda. The last few years of his life are spent in the darkness of some labyrinth where physical sensations are the only realities. All that he lives for is an eggnog with whiskey every two to three hours.

Dorinda's fortunes follow an opposite course to those of Jason, Glasgow's intention being that the betrayed woman would become the victor instead of the victim. The classic situation requires that as a betrayed woman carrying an illegitimate child, Dorinda should seek either forgiveness or vengeance. Narrowly missing the opportunity for the latter, she does neither; instead she looks for a new kind of life. Deciding that there must be something in life besides love she explores new options. In her deep rooted bond with the land she finds a viable substitute. She uses her intelligence, energy and talents in ways her culture does not recognize as acceptable for a woman. Wearing borrowed overalls, funded with borrowed money, Dorinda withdraws from the society that would coerce her, to establish her reputation in the man's world of farming. She uses new methods and knowledge and pours all her physical and emotional resources into the land. Day and night she toils to reclaim the land her father had lost. After ten years of struggle, she is successful. And only then does she return to wearing women's clothes and to attending the church that would have banished her during her pregnancy. Wearing masculine attire does not in any way lessen her femininity. At the age of thirty-three she is still a handsome woman and enters into an unconsummated marriage with Nathan Pedlar. Lavishing all her affection upon his children and Fluvanna, in time she comes to the gentle compassion that marks her as a woman, the recognition that she does not have to abandon the inherent strengths of the feminine, represented by Rose Emily and her mother, before she can succeed. Although she is childless, she is not barren as some critics have alleged.[21] She has known passion, she has conceived. And what she wrests from the generally unyielding land is fruit, success, promise for the future—the opposite of barrenness.

Throughout the novel Dorinda asserts that she is finished with romantic love. During the years of struggle the work was so exacting, and at the end of the day her nerves were so blessedly benumbed by toil, that Dorinda seldom stopped to ask herself if she were satisfied with her lot. She often told herself that there was no regret left in her memory. Yet whenever she heard his name or remembered his existence, her spirit flagged beneath an overpowering sense of futility. She had released from his influence that part of her consciousness which she could control. But "there were innate impulses which were independent of her will or her emotions; and in these blind instincts of her being there were even now occasional flashes of longing." During the day when she was awake,. she could escape him; but at night, when she slept, she would relive the happiest hours that she had spent with him. "Never the pain, never the cruelty of the past; only the beauty and the unforgettable ecstasy came back to her in her dreams." (228) However, she knows that as the years go by, even if the old regrets awaken again, they would come rarely and they would grow weaker. "She would find happiness again. Not the happiness for which she had once longed, but the serenity of mind which is above the conflict of frustrated desires." (408) Endurance and fortitude have enabled her to overcome the worst phase of her life. At the end of the novel we see her middle-aged, without illusions, and able to face life with "clear-eyed wisdom," which told her that the best of life was ahead of her. "Though in a measure destiny had defeated her, for it had given her none of the gifts she had asked of it, still her failure was one of those defeats, she realized, which are victories. At middle age, she faced the future without romantic glamour, but she faced it with integrity of visions." (408)

Many critics have suggested that Glasgow created such a weak character as Jason in order to magnify the female protagonist. However, this is not true. Her representation of his character does not suggest that women's personal and social success must be based on a male downfall. Dorinda has no influence on Jason's life, whereas he is profoundly influential on hers. His first crime is getting involved with Dorinda when he is already engaged to Geneva; his second when he expects Dorinda to carry on a relationship even though he is married. Jason's downfall is inevitable—its seeds are present in his character. Surely Dorinda would have infinitely preferred Jason to be the kind of man she first took him to be. What Glasgow is saying is that no viable relationship is possible between a man who subscribes to the existing double standards of morality and does not have the courage to honour his commitments, and a woman who is strong, inherently independent and capable.

II

After the completion of *Barren Ground*, Glasgow embarked on her great trilogy of Richmond or "Queenborough": *The Romantic Comedians*, *They Stooped to Folly* and *The Sheltered Life*. Of the three, I will be analyzing only two—*The Romantic Comedians* and *The Sheltered Life*—as it is only in these two novels that the theme of this study is consciously dealt with. The books do not constitute a trilogy in the sense that they have a continuous plot or common characters. But, they share a common setting and class (the old but still prosperous Richmond families), and a spirit of ironic high comedy. They also share a hero, at least to the extent that the principal observer in each is an elderly man.

"Turning from *Barren Ground* to *The Romantic Comedians* is like turning from Hardy to Meredith, from *The Return of the Native* to *The Egoist*. It is one of the *tours de force* of American literature."[22] However, *The Romantic Comedians* is not pure comedy. Glasgow herself feared that the "ironic overtones" may seem to deny the tragic mood of the novel. For there is tragedy in the theme, though it is tragedy running, like the "divine things" of Nietzsche, "on light feet."[23] The novel is mainly centred in the consciousness of Judge Gamaliel Honeywell, a distinguished lawyer of aristocratic descent. And it is through his interactions with the two central female figures Amanda and Annabel that his character is delineated.

Unlike Jason, Honeywell is mocked rather than villainized. Through this satirical portrait Glasgow attacks the society that conveniently regards as "nature" in men what it considers "depravity" in women. (7) The double standard of sexual morality that allows a sixty-six year old man to regard himself as a suitable mate for a twenty-three year old girl, whereas by common consent a fifty-eight year old woman must surely have put all thought of romance out of her head, is ironically debunked. Having written with bitterness of betrayed women who learned to live without the happiness of love, she now mocks the fatuous male who thinks polygamous happiness is his prerogative. Glasgow, writing about the theme of *The Romantic Comedians* says: "As for the idea—well, I was worn out with having men write what they know or don't know about dangerous ages in women."[24]

At the age of sixty-five, with the death of his wife Cordelia, Judge Honeywell begins to experience inexplicable but unmistakable longings in his autumnal years for a fulfillment which he had been denied in his youth. The novel opens with the Judge arranging lilies on his former wife's grave, surprised at the physical zest he felt after the year of mourning. Sitting beside the grave he sighs to himself that he is "a bird with a broken wing," only to find disconcertingly that "his broken wing was helplessly trying to flutter."[25] He feels youthful as compared to his friends. The memory of his ninety-year-old father, who had sired twelve children, and the sight of plethoric gentlemen of eighty foxtrotting on spindly legs make him feel "that at sixty-five he was too young to renounce the innocent pleasures of life." (72) Despite his confidence, and despite the "budding and piping and twittering" (2) that is going on in his tempestuous heart, his person is subjected to close, harsh scrutiny. The author's eye does not spare the lean, stiff angularity, the brittle shanks, the veined and desiccated hands, the "mottled stains under the eyes that flowed into the sallow flush of the high cheek-bones, the corded folds of the throat." (3)

Having got the "maggot of youth" (134) into his head, he even deludes himself into believing that he does not look or feel a day older than thirty-five years. He feels remarkably young for his years, "and after all—he had all tradition behind him in his opinion—a man is only as old as his instincts." (49) Like other men he was polygamous by instinct; yet so far he had "confined his impetuous desires within the temperate zone of monogamy." (3) But now there is an "April burgeoning within" which draws him in the direction of sweet young girls, especially twenty-three-year old Annabel Upchurch, one of Cordelia's numerous poor cousins. His recurring sexual reveries are of Annabel's unclad limbs or of "the glimmering ivory shapes of nymphs, who danced on rose-white feet to the music of running water. In spirals and wreaths and garlands, faintly coloured like the earliest spring petals, they spun round him, whirling, drifting, flying, in the wind. . . . Clusters of girls, curving, swaying, bending, advancing, retreating, and always they smiled as they retreated, into the iridescent mist of April." (47) The daydream merges with an actual ball, in which flowerlike girls whirl beguilingly over the dance floor. His fantasies impel him toward the girls of twenty who are caught in the eddying dance, whereas public opinion seems to be firmly pushing him toward the past, toward queenly Amanda Lightfoot.

Amanda, his first love and ideal, was the woman he had adored "to the edge of delirium" in his early youth. She was then, and she remained for twenty years afterward, the crowned belle and beauty of Queenborough. Thirty-seven years ago, for a few blissful months, he had been engaged to her. But a lovers' quarrel had ended it, and while in pursuit of her on board a ship, the "versatile emotions of man had entangled him in an affair with Cordelia" (13) and he had married her. Amanda's queenly pride had prevented her from making the smallest gesture of allurement or revealing by the slightest flicker of an eyelash that he had ruined her life. As the judge reflected complacently, "there was much to be said in favour of the womanly woman. At least men felt safe with her." (14) Secure in this thought, he could at times dwell sympathetically though ponderously upon her frustrated womanhood. "It was, he felt, pathetic, it was even tragic, that she had never known the complete joy of belonging to some good man." Indeed he was willing to make "a heavy sacrifice in order to unite her to any good man in the world except himself." (34) Convinced that a man remains young longer than a woman of the same age, he cannot look upon Amanda as his contemporary, though she is eight years younger than him. For him, she is a well-preserved, grey-haired lady who must have "put the thought of love outside of her life." (58) So far as he is concerned, beautiful women who were no longer young had ceased to interest him, and as he felt like a very young man, he considers it unfair that he should be assigned by the people about him to an elderly woman, and a spinster at that. And so, the more the society of Queenborough tried to push him in the direction of Amanda, the more determined he became every minute that he would refuse to be pushed.

In Amanda Lightfoot, Glasgow skilfully portrayed a woman completely formed by tradition. Somewhat laughably, yet pathetically, Amanda in the post-war age becomes a martyr to concepts of virtue and moral responsibility which have lost the universal respect of even her contemporaries. Almost forty years she has played the role of being Judge Honeywell's ideal, and has made a fetish of being faithful. She is quite divorced from reality, and despite the number of her ardent admirers in the past, she has no real knowledge of men. Annabel is quite right when she points out that women like Amanda have encouraged men to be "morally flabby." However, she really did not have much choice. Linda Wagner aptly comments: "Taught to invest her life in the love of a good man, women like Amanda could only wait to be 'fulfilled.'"[26] On the whole her situation provides genuine pathos. As Glasgow describes her: "Serene, unselfish, with the reminiscence of a vanished day in her face and figure, she belonged to that fortunate generation of women who had no need to think, since everything was decided for them by the feelings of a lady and the Episcopal Church." (143)

The Judge's longing for youthful renewal instead of peace of mind, his fascination for "the unwholesome, the prohibited, and the immoral" draws him toward Annabel. However, he always seeks to justify himself in terms of convention. Unwilling to admit his awakening passion for Annabel, he at first rationalizes his instinctive withdrawal from Amanda as a need to remain faithful to Cordelia's memory. Later, he complacently persuades himself that Annabel needs him more than he needs her. According to him, she requires not only his money and his kindness to recover from her disappointment in love, but being a delicate woman he hopes that she may come to prefer his considerate caresses to the ardour of a youthful man. Moreover, he comically embroiders the actualities of Annabel's nature by continually relaxing the truth in her behalf: she is so pretty, he decides with passion instead of logic, that she cannot help being "good." He always thinks of her charm in terms of wild nature, of "fields and streams," of "tall wind-blown grasses," of the swallow's flight, of the "April mist" in her grey-green eyes, and identifies her with the rose and ivory-coloured nymphs that trouble his imagination. He is unable to see how unsuited she is for the role of matron, especially as she is very free and completely devoid of moral duplicity. The contrast between her outward energy and her coldness toward him he interprets as a sign of maidenly reserve. Totally egocentric, he insists upon thinking of her as innocent and ignorant, and he even fatuously feels that he can mould her nature nearer to his ideal by being her perfect teacher. "Training her tender mind had been, from the beginning of his engagement, one of the delights to which he had looked forward with deep satisfaction." (168)[27] That she is not the placid woman venerated by tradition and society and that she finds him physically repugnant, he fails to perceive for a long time. Masculine blindness and the evasive idealism of the culture which had formed him conspire to keep him ignorant of the truth, though there are moments when he wonders whether his own ideals of the opposite sex are mistaken. When it comes to understanding Annabel, his twin-sister Edmonia's injunction is certainly applicable: that "the wisest man has only the wisdom of a fool when he tries to understand a woman." (87)

Annabel Upchurch, the protagonist, is an intelligent, unconventional and daring young woman. As the Judge realizes, she is "delicate as a flower on the surface . . . but with a vein of iron beneath." (165) Determined to live her own life—her constant refrain is "I want my life"—and not be a "sham," she has no patience with hypocrisy and wonders what is so "moral" about lying. She does not want to be a "true" woman, i.e. conform to the conventional pattern of womanhood, because to her conventional women do not seem to be a bit "real." Fearlessly frank and outspoken, she makes no secret of her disappointment in love and the subsequent heartbreak she suffers. She wonders how women of her mother's generation could "keep alive with things like this bottled up inside of them? If they never talked of them and Mother says they would have died first, they must have let themselves be eaten away in secret." (110) Her unhappy affair with Angus Blount leads her to react adversely towards young men, whom she says she despises, and towards love and romance in general. Naively assuming that money could be a substitute for love, she is tempted to accept the Judge's proposal of marriage. However, her sense of justice and her honesty lead her to question Amanda about her feelings for the Judge before she accepts the proposal. Despite her strong desire to escape from genteel poverty, "she wouldn't take a man away from another woman . . . if he were as rich as Croesus." (131)

Within a few months of her marriage to the Judge, she realizes her folly, and how "immoral" such a marriage can be. Her love for Dabney Birdsong only expedites the denouement. In an impassioned scene she blames her mother and the Judge for taking advantage of her innocence and ignorance about life and propelling her into an "immoral" marriage. The vein of iron in her, will not allow her to be subdued and in spite of her mother's and husband's implorings, she elopes with Dabney. Mrs. Upchurch reflecting upon the disastrous outcome of her daughter's marriage and voicing the opinion of her society, is inclined to blame Annabel: "In the earlier generations, how many girls had married men old enough to be their fathers or grandfathers, and yet nothing disastrous had come out of it, nothing at least, with which husbands, aided by duty or the fear of living, had not been able to deal. Women had known then how to live without love, just as they had known how to live without beauty or happiness." (300) She strongly feels, and so does the conventional society, that her daughter "ought to have sacrificed her feeling to her duty." (338) However, the author's sympathies are with Annabel who escapes any real criticism for her actions. Not only does she allow her to live her own life, but she lets her find love and happiness.

In the end, it is the Judge who emerges as the most ridiculous and pathetic figure in the novel. In Judge Honeywell's prostration of himself before Annabel, there is indignity and morbidity. Mrs. Upchurch's view of the Judge dominates in the novel: "Could anything, she asked herself, be more unmanly than an elderly man in the clutch of an emotional crisis?" (227) One would have expected that the debacle of his relationship with Annabel would have had a sobering influence on him. But after a period of illness, we see him on the verge of committing the same folly once again. The sight of the cool and fresh young nurse stirs up the same desires, and his last thought is: "Spring is here, and I am feeling almost as young as I felt last year." (346)

Through the characterization of Judge Honeywell, Glasgow

gives vent to her wrath, and seeks to puncture and punish the vanity of the patriarchal male. Her ironic sense of the disparity existing between the conventional views that men have regarding women, and the reality (which gives rise to serious problems in man-woman relationships) is given effective expression in this novel. Glasgow's ideal male figure would certainly be devoid of the double standards (that allow a man to fall in love even with one foot in the grave, but debar a woman from giving expression to her emotional needs) and the vanity which are so evident in Gamaliel Honeywell and are the product of a patriarchal culture.

III

The Sheltered Life, the last of her tragicomedies of manners is her finest and most intense achievement. In this novel, Glasgow employed two points of view. "Age and youth look on the same scene, the same persons, the same events and occasions, the same tragedy in the end. . . . Nothing happens that is not seen, on one side, through the steady gaze of the old man, seeing life as it is, and, on the other side, by the troubled eyes of the young girl, seeing life as she would wish it to be."[28] It is through the consciousness of General David Archbald and his grand-daughter, Jenny Blair Archbald, that the entire action is filtered. However, General Archbald is not merely an onlooker.. Although there is a suppressed rebellious side to him, he by and large subscribes to, and is the spokesman for the idealism and the moral code of his society, something that Glasgow criticizes. And Jenny is intimately involved in the tragedy that occurs in the novel. In fact the entire novel revolves around George Birdsong, the male protagonist, and his relationship with his wife Eva, and the young girl, Jenny.

George Birdsong, a struggling young lawyer, is a handsome and charming person, but extremely ineffectual. He is kind hearted and generous to a fault. For example, the General can never forget that, when George had inherited a small fortune, he had offered it to him to help him over a moment of financial crisis; a little later George had just as readily frittered it away in bad investments. Like Jason Greylock he is neither mean nor evil; he is simply weak and careless. Having married Eva, the reigning belle of Queenborough, he finds it too great a strain to be worthy of so idealized a being as his wife. As he himself admits to the nine-year-old Jenny, he "was born with a roving nature."[29] And his roving nature leads him into having casual encounters with younger, less charming, but easily approachable girls such as Della Barron, or the mulatto washerwoman, Memoria. In his own way, George loves his wife Eva, but his way does not include fidelity of mind or body. As Mrs. Archbald puts it: "There have been so many things in his life that have had nothing to do with his marriage." (97) Although he would never deliberately hurt her and could give every drop of his blood for her, he yet never tries to curb his "roving nature." This is mainly because he feels no necessity to do so. The society sanctions his double standards of sexual morality. According to General Archbald, "Those other things . . . have nothing to do with his marriage. . . . All that side of his life has no more to do with his devotion to Eva than if—than if it were malaria from the bite of a mosquito." (97) Musing upon George and Eva's relationship he cannot help but feel that "life would be more agreeable if women could realize that man is not a monogamous animal, and that even a man in love does not necessarily wish to love all the time." (101) He is convinced that there would be less unhappiness in the world if "good women could either accept or reject the moral nature of man." (101) In order to justify himself George chooses biology as an alibi, and uses this to explain his various escapes from responsibility through sport, women and drink.

Eva Birdsong was "one of those celebrated beauties who, if they still exist, have ceased to be celebrated. . . . For the first five years of the eighteen nineties, she had gathered the hearts of men . . . in her hands." (15) Moreover, she had been endowed with a singing voice so pure in quality that many, including Eva herself, believed that she could have had a grand career in opera. However, she had tossed aside all her triumphs, and given up all prospects of a career when she married George Birdsong, the least eligible of her suitors. George's liberality, his uncalculating impulsiveness, and his magnetism are repeatedly stressed throughout the novel in order to render credible Eva Birdsong's initial infatuation with him and her continued loyalty to him, despite his inability to remain faithful to her. As she tells the General, George's heroic feat as a boy had won her heart: he had rushed into a burning house to save a Negro child, Memoria, who years later was to become his mistress.

Throughout the novel Eva is framed with admiring looks—women hang from their windows to watch her walk past, party goers circle her as she waltzes with George. Eva is beauty, womanliness, perfection—in short she is the embodiment of society's and George's ideals. Having been elevated to this position, she is determined to play her role to perfection, even if it means deluding herself about George's true character and keeping up the pretense of a harmonious relationship with him. Mrs. Archbald shrewdly remarks: "I am perfectly sure that if she knew everything, she would never betray herself. When happiness failed her, she would begin to live on pride, which wears better. Keeping up an appearance is more than a habit with Eva. It is a second nature." (19) Ever since her marriage, she has lived with "the necessity to justify her sacrifice to herself—perhaps to the world. To have given up all that—and she really believes that she gave up a career in grand opera, for anything less than a great passion would seem inexcusable." (21-22) To sustain this romantic alibi she must keep affirming her faith in the "great passion" of her marriage, which requires that she always try to believe that George still loves her completely and Eva almost wills herself to believe this. As she tells the General, "If I hadn't believed that he loved me, I couldn't have borne it." (14) Ironically, she makes this avowal while George is having his first significant encounter with the maturing Jenny Blair. Implicitly accepting the double standard which condones George's philandering she says: "As long as there is love . . . a woman can forgive anything. A man can be amused in strange ways, I understand that, though some women cannot." (141)

Eva Birdsong goes through life with a perfect smile on her face and never complains until her health, her life itself is threatened. Her consciously contrived artifice has been made necessary by the life of pretense she has led so long. John Welch, her young cousin and a doctor, asserts that part of her trouble is a wounded spirit, since she has never known a natural moment in her marriage: "I honestly believe, . . . that she has never drawn a natural breath since she was married. If she dies . . . it will be the long pretense of her life that has killed her." (153) As Glasgow's spokesman in the novel, John Welch's cynicism acts as a corrective to the idealism of the Queenborough society and the code of perfect behaviour by which they live. In sharp, direct language he strikes at the root of Eva's illness: "I sometimes think the whole trouble is too much George. George is not a restful person to live with. . . . That is a part, the larger part probably, of the trouble. Think what it must have cost her to keep up being an ideal for more than twenty years! You may talk about keeping up socially, but it doesn't touch the effort of keeping up emotionally. She must have known, too, in her heart, at least, that George wasn't worth it." (199)

Linda Wagner insightfully comments: "Eva's tragedy as person is that she has accepted the illusion of woman's suitable role: she has become the perfect wife, only and exclusively the perfect wife."[30] So strong is her belief in the validity of her position that she advises Jenny: "Well, you will understand still better when you are older. You will know then that a great love doesn't leave room for anything else in a woman's life. It is everything. . . . You can never give up too much for happiness." (55, 57) It is some eight years later, when a serious operation leaves her, in George's phrase, "a maimed woman," and her beauty is tarnished, that she realizes that she has failed both in keeping her husband and in finding herself, and she warns Jenny: "Whatever you do, Jenny Blair, never risk all your happiness on a singe chance. Always keep something back, if it is only a crumb. Always keep something back for a rainy day." (271) Giving up all for love is to become a slave to fear. "Fear of losing love. Fear of losing the power that won love so easily. I sometimes think that there is nothing so terrible for a woman . . . as to be loved for her beauty." (209) In a moment of rare honesty she admits to Jenny that she has lived an unnatural life for the last forty years, and that she is "worn out with being somebody else—with somebody's ideal." (285)

Linda Wagner rightly points out that the protagonist of the novel is not Eva, but Jenny Blair. Making effective use of irony, Glasgow depicts Jenny in the opening chapter as the antithesis of the female characters of Alcott's *Little Women*. Jenny refuses to model her character on Jo or Meg; instead she insists on her right to individualism: "I'm different, I'm different. . . . I'm alive, alive, alive, and I'm Jenny Blair Archbald." (3) Her desire to be "different" and independent continues unabated till her adolescence. When her mother wants her to "come out" at the age of eighteen, she rebels. Instead of conforming to society's expectations of her, she declares, much like Annabel, that she wants to live her own life. She would like to go to New York and study to be an actress. Unfortunately she receives little encouragement from either her family or the society; nor is there any independent, achieving woman among her acquaintances whom she can emulate: And so, as everyone around her worships Eva, she follows suit, and Eva comes to embody for her order, beauty, perfection, an unattainable ideal of living. When she chooses Eva as her model, she begins the pattern that dooms her. Having been brought up in an extremely sheltered environment, and shielded from contact with life she is extremely naive and slightly irresponsible as well. Added to that she is also daring, "and that quality implicates her on several occasions with George Birdsong—first when she is a child on roller skates, surprising him at the home of his mulatto mistress; later in his garden; and subsequently in the hospital garden." In all these encounters, Jenny "accepts the male duplicity, the double standard: George has relationships with women besides his wife."[31] Jenny accepts George's philandering because the double standard is an accepted part of Queenborough life. She is not, as F.P.W. McDowell claims "an amoral young girl in whom the sheltered life has encouraged an idle hedonism and a compulsive desire to satisfy her instincts."[32] It is just that her vital energy has not been channelised properly. Her faulty upbringing has made her like any other young girl of her time, an extremely "self-centered being," so that she is "like every other young girl who has grown up without coming in touch with the world." She is so "bottled up inside" that her "imagination has turned into a hothouse for sensation." (250) Glasgow's sympathies are certainly with Jenny. Marcelle Thiebaux is surely wrong in saying that "Jenny Blair, the independent girl who accepts her sexuality, who rejects the role of the Southern *debutante*, who wants to do something with her life . . . is made to pursue a shallow, treacherous course."[33]

In spite of knowing full well that Jenny is just an innocent young girl, and that he is old enough to be her father, George enters into a relationship with her and that too at a time when he professes to be miserable on account of his wife's illness. In a moment of honesty he admits to the General that Eva has never been happy with him, but he seeks to exonerate himself on the plea that he is a weak man:

> It was all too big for me, that was the trouble, what she is, what she feels, what she thinks, what she expects—everything. I am not worth her little finger. Nobody need tell me that. But, after all, you can't make a man bigger than he really is. I know I'm not a big man, and when I come up against anything that is too much for me, beauty, goodness, unhappiness, I give way inside. I can't stand but so much of a thing, and then I break up, and that's all there is of me. When that happens I am obliged to get out of it. Anywhere. No matter which way sport, women, drink. No matter. (185)

The denouement occurs when Eva finds her husband embracing Jenny, her young friend and protegee. With an energy born of desperation she brings an end to her long life of pretense by shooting him. Only at this juncture does she manage to break out of the stereotype. However, since her entire identity has been as George's wife, all that remains for her is emptiness: "Jenny looked at Mrs. Birdsong, who sat very erect, and gazed, with her fixed smile, into the twilight beyond the window. Her face was so vacant that her expression and even her features were like wax." (290)

Ironically, none of the characters is able to assess the significance of what happens, which prompted Marcelle Thiebaux to call the work "a dark satire rather than a tragedy."[34] Glasgow's aim in this novel is to offer a critique of the existing patriarchal society. It is a society that sanctions philandering on the part of men and offers no career options for women. With many likable qualities, George Birdsong has one trait that is responsible for wrecking his wife's life and happiness and, to a certain extent, deflecting Jenny from her chosen path of pursuing a career.

NOTES

1. Ellen Glasgow, *A Certain Measure* (New York: Harcourt, Brace and Company, 1938), p. 12.
2. Maxwell Geismar, *Rebels and Ancestors: The American Novel, 1890-1915* (Boston: Houghton Mifflin Company, 1953), p. 219.
3. Reference may be made to Edith Wharton's novels, especially *The Age of Innocence* where she strongly criticizes this. Glasgow's novel *The Sheltered Life* also provides a similar critique.
4. Cited in Linda M. Wagner, *Ellen Glasgow: Beyond Convention* (Austin: University of Texas Press, 1982), p. 4.
5. Glasgow, *A Certain Measure*, p. vii.
6. Ellen Glasgow, *The Woman Within* (New York: Harcourt, Brace and Company, 1954), p. 108.
7. Glasgow, *A Certain Measure*, p. 9.
8. Geismar, p. 220.
9. Note dated 1910, in Glasgow Papers. Quoted in E. Stanley Godbold Jr., Ellen Glasgow and *The Woman Within* (Baton

Rouge: Louisiana State University Press, 1972), p. 92.

10. Louis Auchincloss, *Pioneers and Caretakers: A Study of Nine American Women Novelists* (1961; rpt. Minneapolis; University of Minnesota Press, 1965), pp. 88-90.
11. Godbold, p. 151.
12. Blair Rouse, "Ellen Glasgow's Civilized Men," in M. Thomas Inge, ed., *Ellen Glasgow: Centennial Essays* (Virginia: University Press of Virginia, 1976), pp. 133-34.
13. Emily Clark, "Appreciation of Ellen Glasgow and Her Work," *Virginia Quarterly Review*, V (1929).
14. Glasgow, "Preface to the Romantic Comedians." Quoted in *Louis Auchincloss, Pioneers and Caretakers*, p. 77.
15. Glasgow, "Preface" to *Barren Ground* (1933; rpt. New York: Hill and Wang, 1958), p. vi.
16. Glasgow, Letters, pp. 74, 107, 69. Quoted in Linda M. Wagner, "*Barren Ground*'s Vein of Iron: Dorinda Oakley and Some Concepts of the Heroine in 1925," *Mississippi Quarterly*, 32 (1979), 559.
17. Glasgow, *A Certain Measure*, p. 19.
18. Ellen Glasgow, *Barren Ground* (1925, 1933; rpt. New York: Hill and Wang, 1968), p. 51. All further references will be to this edition of the book and shall be incorporated in the text.
19. Godbold, p. 137.
20. Wayne Lesser, "The Problematic of Regionalism and the Dilemma of Glasgow's *Barren Ground*," *Southern Literary Journal*, 11, No. 2 (1979), p. 13.
21. Louis D. Rubin Jr., *No Place on Earth* (Austin: University of Texas Press, 1959), p. 26. He comments: "Dorinda's life is a progressive espousal of barrenness. She is not fruitful."
22. Auchincloss, p. 77.
23. Glasgow, *A Certain Measure*, p. 223.
24. Glasgow, *Letters*, p. 90. Quoted in Linda M. Wagner, *Ellen Glasgow: Beyond Convention*, p. 83.
25. Ellen Glasgow, *The Romantic Comedians* (New York: A.L. Burt Company, 1926), p. 1. All further references to the book will be incorporated in the text.
26. Linda M. Wagner, *Ellen Glasgow: Beyond Convention*, p. 83.
27. Reference may be made to Edith Wharton's heroes who exhibit a similar desire.
28. Glasgow, *A Certain Measure*, pp. 200-1.

29. Ellen Glasgow, *The Sheltered Life* (1938; rpt. New York: Hill and Wang, 1979), p. 48. All subsequent references will be to this edition of the book and shall be incorporated in the text.
30. Linda M. Wagner, *Ellen Glasgow: Beyond Convention*, p. 86.
31. *Ibid.*, p. 87.
32. F.P.W. McDowell, *Ellen Glasgow and the Ironic Art of Fiction* (Madison: University of Wisconsin Press, 1963), p. 186
33. Marcelle Thiebaux, *Ellen Glasgow* (New York: Frederick Ungar Publishing Company, 1982), p. 152.
34. Thiebaux, p. 149.

The Little Male: Willa Cather's Protagonist

There is an interesting anecdote about Willa Cather's advent in the University of Nebraska. A fellow student recalled her arrival in class. The door opened and a head with short hair and a straw hat appeared. A deep voice inquired if this were the Greek class. Someone nodded. The door opened wider and a girl entered, amidst peals of laughter. This incident reveals a great deal about Willa Cather's life and her attitude to it.

Born in 1873 in Virginia into a family that had been farmers since the eighteenth century, Willa Cather was unconventional and rebellious even as a child. Edith Lewis, Cather's friend and companion for almost forty years, recalls how Willa once told of an old judge who had called on the family. When he began stroking her curls and talking to her in the platitudes one addressed to little girls, Willa horrified her mother by breaking out suddenly: "I'se a dang'ous nigger, I is."[1] It was really an attempt to break through the unreal conventions about little girls and it was the only way that occurred to her at the moment. As a young girl, Willa shocked her friends and neighbours in the small town of Red Cloud in Nebraska (where her family had migrated) by dressing like a boy—she wore starched shirts, ties, hats; sported a boyish haircut and even carried a cane on occasion. She preferred to be called "Will" or "Willie," and it gave her a particular satisfaction when a perceptive, appreciative person would call her Dr. Will. Taking an unfeminine, precocious interest in surgery and even embalming, at the age of fourteen she stated that her "idea of perfect happiness"[2] was amputating limbs. She decided that she wanted to be a doctor and pursued her vocation seriously, making house calls with two Red Cloud physicians, and on one occasion administering chloroform while one of them amputated a boy's leg. This hobby, along with her preference for the conversation of unusual older men to most of the pleasures sought by the other boys and girls, and the dangerous opinions she held about religion, made her an alien in that small town.

Many critics have commented on this aspect of Cather's personality—namely, her desire to deny her womanhood. James Woodress, her biographer, attributes it to a "strong masculine element rooted deep in her personality."[3] What is perhaps nearer to the truth is that, having been born into the sociocultural milieu of the nineteenth century, Willa Cather early in life realized that achieving in the world was a male prerogative. Passivity, lack of assertiveness and energy, and the consequent loss of possibility of achievement, were traditionally the lot of the female. From childhood Willa was determined to achieve. Because she had a clear understanding of nineteenth century sex roles, she exhibited a marked preference for "male" activities, and tried to deny the womanhood that prohibited the achievement she passionately sought. The identity conflict that Cather suffered is an example of the woman writer experiencing "her gender as a painful obstacle, or even a debilitating inadequacy."[4]

Although Willa Cather never joined any woman's movement or took part in suffragist marches like Glasgow, she was a feminist to the core. Her feminist bias is reflected in her life style as well as in her writings. Determined to be a professional writer as well as economically independent, she set about her task single-mindedly. Much has been made of her decision to remain single in spite of the opportunities she had for marrying. James Woodress discusses this at length and then concludes: "It seems perfectly clear that she simply had no need for heterosexual relationships; she was married to her art."[5] Deborah G. Lambert plainly states that "Cather was a lesbian who could not, or did not acknowledge her homosexuality."[6] Certainly Cather was a committed artist. She was also intensely conscious of what seemed to her a serious anomaly:

being a serious writer and being a woman. This consciousness was enhanced by her awareness of the fact that as a woman, and a married one at that, society would expect her to play certain roles which would prove to be inimical to her as an artist. Given the conventional expectations that men had of women, it was perhaps too much to expect a man to accept and understand her role as a professional writer. Hence her decision not to marry, to retain the liberty she had grown enamoured of, and to lavish her deepest affections on the women who played a supporting role in her life as an artist. She once observed to Elizabeth Shepley Sergeant: "One must have the power to refuse most of the rest of life . . . to be free, to work at [my] table—that *is* [emphasis Cather's] all in all. . . . There are fates and fates but one cannot live them all. Some would call mine servitude but I call it liberation. Miss Jewett too turned away from marriage."[7]

Cather's determination to succeed as a writer rather than as a woman writer prompted her to ignore the advice of Sarah Orne Jewett, who told her that when a woman tried to write from a man's point of view, she inevitably falsified.[8] She successfully adopted a male persona, Jim Burden, in *My Antonia*, and in *A Lost Lady* the entire action is seen through the eyes of a young man, Niel Herbert. However, they are not her spokesmen as is often believed. In fact, through them she provides a critique of the cultural myths about women. Although her male characters are convincing portraits, they are overshadowed by her female protagonists, a fact that has been noted by many. According to J.J. Murphy: "The Cather male is a little male, worried about what people say and guilty of snobbery. . . . He puts his faith in idealizations of reality, especially in the women he makes responsible for upholding the ideals he creates."[9] James Woodress remarks: "It is true . . . that most of her great characters are female: Alexandra Bergson, Antonia, Thea Kronborg, Marian Forester."[10] Carl Van Doren comments: "Alexandra Bergson in *O Pioneers!*, Thea Kronborg in *The Song of the Lark*, Antonia Shimerda in *My Antonia*—around these as girls and as women the actions primarily revolve. It is not, however, as other Helens or

Gudruns that they affect their universes; they are not darlings of heroes but heroes themselves."[11] And Susan Rosowski, writing about Cather's women, notes: "Willa Cather created a gallery of powerful women. It includes the indomitable pioneer Alexandra Bergson, the great artist Thea Kronborg, the Earth Mother Antonia Shimerda, the artful teacher of civilized standards Marian Forester, the fiercely individual Myra Driscoll Henshawe."[12] These women have the strength to act independently of cultural expectations that a woman exist as an object to a male perspective, to break through the conventional roles imposed upon them. On the other hand, the male protagonists are "fastidiously conservative men" who "flounder, confused and weak in a time of change, retreating further and further into a self-contained world of abstract beauty, strenuously creating a past that never existed."[13]

Given the nature of Cather's male and female protagonists, it is but natural that in her novels, love between man and woman is never a source of ultimate satisfaction. This has been seen as a limitation of her art and an inability on her part which is to be regretted. James Woodress comments: "It is a rare novel or story of hers in which there is not an unhappy marriage either at the core or the periphery of the work."[14] And John H. Randall notes that her novels abound with examples of "frustrating and unhappy marriages. . . . This imposing array of evidence reveals Willa Cather as interested in showing that permanently satisfying relationships between men and women are impossible. Of course this is highly idiosyncratic; she seems bent on justifying her own way of life rather than portraying the world as it is."[15] It is my contention that the absence of viable man-woman relationships in Cather's fiction is not a limitation or an idiosyncracy. Rather, it is perhaps intentional, as she could not conceive of the possibility of satisfactory relationships between men who were weak and convention bound, and women who were strong, independent and unconventional. Further, I would like to suggest that through the negative portraits of these male characters, Cather is perhaps projecting her ideal image of man.

Unlike Edith Wharton and Ellen Glasgow, Cather did not involve her characters in truly dramatic relations with each other. In other words, her men and women are never "lovers" in the true sense of the term. This aspect of her writing is a direct reflection of her conviction that strong and achieving women were not likely to find suitable mates and hence the need to look for alternate modes of fulfillment.

I

The Song of the Lark is Cather's *Kunstlerroman*, her story of an "artist's awakening and struggle; her floundering escape from a smug, domestic, self-satisfied provincial world of utter ignorance."[16] The novel grew out of Cather's intense preoccupation with opera at that time and her admiration for and interest in the complex personality of Olive Fremstad, a Swedish-American opera singer. However, as Edith Lewis in *Willa Cather Living* has taken pains to point out, Thea Kronborg, the heroine of the novel, is not a direct portrait of Fremstad. Many other elements enter into the character, especially much of Willa Cather's own childhood and youth.

Of the four men who play a rather significant role in Thea's growth as an artist, there is only one with whom she gets emotionally involved. Fred Ottenburg, a beer prince, was what people called an "imaginative businessman."[17] He was the third son of the big brewer in St. Lewis, greatly indulged by his mother and had "never wanted anything that he could not have it." (354) Full of life and energy, he had never been bored for a single day in his life. "He had so many natural interests that he had no affectations. Physical energy was the thing he was full to the brim of, and music was one of its natural forms of expression. He had a healthy love of sport and art, of eating and drinking. When he was in Germany, he scarcely knew where the soup ended and the symphony began." (354) In short, he had, as Thea soon realized, "some go in him." (352)

Thea, on the other hand, has grown up in Moonstone, a small Midwestern town; in a family of seven children. Even as a child, Thea with her "fierce little mouth, and her delicate, tender chin" (12) had been different from other children. Her mother found her more interesting than the rest of the children and took her more seriously; her maiden aunt Tillie intuitively knew that Thea was different from the other Kronborgs and her romantic imagination often built up brilliant futures for her niece. Thea herself was aware "that there was something about her that was different. But it was more like a friendly spirit than like anything that was a part of herself. She brought everything to it, and it answered her; happiness consisted of that backward and forward movement of herself." (100)

Convinced that Thea is an unusual child, Howard Archie, the family doctor and the first of the several males who come to her aid, lends her his books, takes her on his rounds, and talks seriously with her. More important, he encourages her ambition, solemnly telling her: "You're going to Chicago some day and do something with that fine voice of yours. You're going to be a number one musician and make us proud of you." (176) By the time Thea is sixteen, she does not need Doctor Archie to tell her that the "people who forge ahead and do something" are the ones who "really count." (176)

Professor A. Wunsch, Thea's alcoholic childhood piano teacher, is the first person to recognise her talent, and he also feeds her ambition. From the beginning Wunsch realizes that Thea Kronborg is unlike the other complacent young girls whom he teaches and who drive him to rage. Rather than try to "get something for nothing," as the other girls do, she sets herself to her lessons with a doggedness that tempts the itinerant teacher to cherish hopes for her. The fact that she has "a rugged will as well as imagination" (37) is what initially impresses him and compels him to believe in her. Over the years the two of them come to share an unspoken secret: the understanding that Thea would one day "leave them all behind." It is significant that Wunsch's name in German means desire, because that is his most valuable gift to Thea. It is he who teaches her to desire, who tells her earnestly: "Nothing is far and nothing is near, if one desires. The world is little, people are little. There is only one big thing—desire." (95) When he is forced to flee Moonstone after disgracing himself on a drunken spree, he leaves behind him a legacy to Thea: a battered score of Gluck's opera Orpheus, the first great music she has ever seen.

The third man who discerns that Thea "is developing something fine" (74) and comes to her aid in her struggle for success is Ray Kennedy, a freight conductor on the run between Moonstone and Denver. At thirty Ray dreams of marrying the Reverend Peter Kronborg's youngest daughter as soon as she is old enough. "He believed that in Thea's yellow head he had found his ideal, and that by the time she was old enough to marry, he would be able to keep her like a queen." (67) However, he has no clear idea of what is going on in her head, and as Thea realizes, he does not, for even a single instant, understand her. Yet he has unquestioning faith in Thea's ability to achieve something great. After he is killed in a train wreck, it is discovered that he has insured his life for six hundred dollars in Thea's favour—to be used for travelling to Chicago to study music. Thus he enables her to escape from the smug, provincial world of Moonstone, and from the fear of the tongue, that terror of little towns. Even at the height of her career, Thea remembers that she began life on six hundred dollars, the price of a man's life, and it is always a sobering thought.

Often Peter Kronborg's assessment of his daughter has been taken as evidence of the fact that Thea is totally insusceptible to masculine attention and has no need for emotional relationships with the opposite sex. But, when he says that Thea is "not the marrying kind" because she is "too peppery and too fond of having her own way," (129) he is just giving expression to the values held by his society. A woman was supposed to be weak and submissive. Strong and independent women made "good church-workers and missionaries and school-teachers," but not "good wives," (129) the reason being that such women did not conform to male expectations of a "womanly woman."

Alone in Chicago and studying music, Thea becomes more

fully aware of her nature as an artist. She also realizes that her art is a process of self-discovery.

> Her voice, more than any other part of her, had to do with that confidence, that sense of wholeness and inner well-being that she had felt at moments ever since she could remember. . . . She took it for granted that some day, when she was older, she would know a great deal more about it. It was as if he had an appointment to meet the rest of herself sometime, somewhere. It was moving to meet her and she was moving to meet it. (272)

Thea's awakening to herself as an artist is revealed in the Jules Breton painting "The Song of the Lark" in which a peasant girl, on her way to work at dawn, stops to listen to a lark singing over the fields. Thea's sympathetic and intelligent piano teacher, Andor Harsanyi, also directs her toward self-discovery as an artist when he urges her to study voice instead of the piano. Like Wunsch, he also is impressed by Thea's unusual "power of work." (270) And it is while she is taking singing lessons from Madison Bowers that she first meets Fred Ottenburg who is to play such a crucial role in her life. Fred is attracted to Thea because he is "interested in talent," (344) and he recognizes in Thea the raw ingredients of a great artist. She "was something that couldn't be dimmed or downed." She always shot off "like a rifle ball." (392) and did not "lose her nerve in a tight place." (406) Fred has "a way of floating people out of dull or awkward situations, out of their own torpor or constraint or discouragement," (336) and he succeeds in drawing Thea out of her shell in a way that nobody in Chicago had been able to do. Soon she realizes that Fred "was not one of those people who made her spine like a steel rail. On the contrary, he made [her] venturesome." (338) Lonely and starved for emotional and intellectual companionship, it is but natural that Thea should respond to the interest he manifests in her. He not only introduces her into the best musical circles of Chicago, but also caters to a much more mundane need—he provides her with good and nourishing food when she cannot afford it herself. For the first time Thea feels really cared for and becomes dependent on someone. After having had a string of teachers and friends who were old, it was pleasant to have a male friend who was not only young, but intelligent and attractive as well. She soon discovers that she "want[s] him for a sweetheart." (358) And so, when he offers to send her for a holiday to a ranch he owns in Arizona called Panther Canyon, she quite readily agrees, for she sees it as evidence that he cares for her. On her part she knew that she "liked Fred better than anyone else in the world." (381)

Inevitably, their intimacy grows with Fred's arrival at the ranch. Their relationship is unconventional insofar as it does not involve the submission of one to the other. It is more like a camaraderie, they are equals in all respects. Thea admires Ottenburg's physical energy and vies with him at throwing stones in discus fashion; to Henry Biltmer, the lodge keeper, they look like two boys moving about nimbly on the cliffs. As Thea puts it, in Moonstone being in love "meant sitting in a hammock with somebody. I don't want to sit in a hammock with you, but I want to do almost everything else." (403) Similarly, the idea of having a comfortable flat in Chicago, a summer camp up in the woods, musical evenings, and a family to bring up, seems "perfectly hideous" (394) to her. More than anything else, Thea views her relationship with Fred as one of companionship, intellectual as well as emotional. She would like it to be one in which both of them are free to follow their respective careers. And in Fred she believes that she has found a man who would be able to understand and appreciate her aspirations. To a certain extent she is right. As Fred himself admits, rather conceitedly, he is not one of those "jolly fellows" who "want to be the animating force" in a relationship. He cannot think of any other man "who would know what she was driving at—or care. The clever ones were selfish, the kindly ones were stupid." (423)

But Fred is also one of those people who are of the opinion that with girls "who had careers to follow, a young man might have pleasant friendships without being regarded as a prospective suitor or lover." (421) Because Thea is obviously a serious artist, he, like her father, concludes that she is "distinctly not the marrying kind" (421) and so he allowed himself more liberty in his relationship with her. In this respect he is not different from the other young men of his time who have a certain preconceived notion of the "womanly woman" and the woman who is the "marrying kind." And Thea belies the cultural expectations that a woman act according to a male perspective.

Fred fosters the growing intimacy in more ways than one. For example, he frankly admits that although he has had many relationships in the past, he has "never been so much engrossed before." (403) Yet he continues to be rather flippant at times and insists on regarding Thea as an unsentimental person, one who never does "a single thing without an ulterior motive" (391) and himself as an "instrument." Even when Thea makes it obvious to him that she is in earnest and is even contemplating marriage, he encourages her and does not think of revealing to her an important fact about himself—that he is already married to a hysterical woman who will never consent to a divorce. He entices her to Mexico and into a liaison and tries to justify his action to himself.

> "In any case, I shall help her more than I shall hurt her," he kept saying to himself. He admitted that it was not the only motive which impelled him, but it was one of them. "I'll make it my business in life to get her on. There's nothing else I care about so much as seeing her have her chance. She hasn't touched her real force yet. She isn't even aware of it. There isn't one of them that has such a depth to draw from. She'll be one of the great artists of our time. . . . I'll get her off to Germany this winter, or take her. . . . I'll make it up to her, all right." (413)

He admits that his own conduct looked crooked, but consoles himself with the thought that "between men and women, all ways were . . . more or less crooked." (424)

When Thea eventually gets to know of Fred's duplicity, she is heart-broken. However, once the initial shock is over, she sets about, calmly and with characteristic determination, charting her future course of action. What is most apparent to her is that because she has become very dependent on Fred, she must get as far away as possible from him. As she also wants to pursue her profession, Germany is the most obvious choice. She refuses to accept any money from Fred as in that way he would simply be "keeping" her. (445) She tries to excuse his behaviour to herself. But, when he feels hurt at the fact that she is ready to borrow money from Dr. Archie rather than from him, she quietly tells him: "But when you arranged with yourself to take me in like that, you couldn't have been thinking very kindly of me. I can't understand how you carried it through, when I was so easy, and all the circumstances were so easy." (442) Attempting to justify his behaviour to Thea he says: "I honestly could not imagine that words, names, meant so much to you." (442-43) However, he only succeeds in presenting himself in a worse light than before—as one who thinks that in spite of the fact that he is married, he can have a liaison with Thea and that she would be willing. He is also revealed as subscribing to the prevailing double standards of sexual morality. Thea, in her characteristic forthright manner makes it clear to him that the "name" does make a difference to her and that "being married is one thing and not being married is the other thing, and that's all there is to it." (445)

So far as Thea is concerned there is no question of there being anybody else in her life. As she tells Fred many years later, "In a way, I've always been married to you. I'm not very flexible; never was and never shall be. You caught me young. I could never have that over again." (558) However, she does not allow this disappointment to wreck her life. She devotes herself wholeheartedly to her profession and ten years later we see her at the peak of her career—a famous opera singer. Cather renders the necessary isolation and impersonality of the artist with great skill. Thea no longer has a life apart from the opera. A certain remoteness now invests her personality and she has lost much of the spontaneity and energy she once exuded. Fred Ottenburg rightly perceives that only the challenge of her art brings back her vitality and zest for life: "It was only under such excitement, he reflected, that she was entirely illuminated, or wholly present. At other times there was something a little cold and empty, like a big room with no people in it." (533) That she is really lonely is apparent from her remark to Fred: "I'd like to have somebody human to make a report to once in a while." (559)

Although Fred and Thea continue to be friends, very little of the former passion survives. And so, when we are told in the epilogue about their marriage, it is hardly convincing. The action of the novel does not lead up to it, and it almost seems as if Cather tried to force a neat end which is rather incongruous. In any event there is no suggestion that it even remotely approximates the kind of marriage that Thea at one time envisaged.

In this novel as in many others, Cather shows that satisfactory relationships between men and women cannot exist unless men transcend conventional views regarding women, especially if the women are independent and achievement-oriented. Fred Ottenburg has many qualities that make him an agreeable and attractive suitor, but he lacks the most essential ones. First, he subscribes to the prevalent notion that artists and professionally inclined women in general, were not the "marrying kind." Secondly, he, like many of Wharton and Glasgow heroes, considers it a male prerogative to have extra-marital relationships and even has the effrontery to imagine that unconventional women like Thea would readily accede to such liaisons. Given all these factors, it is inevitable that the relationship between Fred and Thea should be unsatisfactory.

II

My Antonia is the novel that immediately followed *The Song of the Lark*. In this novel Cather discarded the conventional plot. Instead of the phase by phase development of

Thea Kronborg, in *My Antonia* there is "a gallery of pictures"[18] which at first glance appear to be arranged in an episodical fashion, but which in reality illuminate one another and contribute to a general tone. *My Antonia* is not a novel in the strict sense of the term and Cather never intended it to be one. As she made it clear, in this book "she was gathering her memories of some persons and places very dear to her, and as she was a writer of stories the memories had taken a narrative form."[19] The memories centred around Annie Sadilek whom Cather had known as a child. She was a Bohemian hired girl who worked for one of Cather's neighbours and who was "'one of the truest artists I ever knew in the keenness and sensitiveness of her enjoyment, in her love of people, and in her willingness to take pains.'"[20] Many years later, during one of her visits to Red Cloud, she again saw Annie, now Annie Pavelka, on her farm surrounded by her large brood of children. The sight recalled memories of her childhood, and the idea for the novel was born.

This is the first novel in which Cather uses a male narrator. However, Jim Burden, the persona, is not Cather's spokesman as some have believed. In fact, Jim has been seen as Cather's "alter ego" and critics have noted the autobiographical elements in Jim Burden's character. For example, John P. Hinz says:

> The parallels between Willa Cather's experience and Jim Burden's are readily recognizable: the narrator, Jim, when ten years old, is sent from Virginia to his grandfather's farm in Nebraska; . . . after three years on the farm, the family moves to the nearby town of Black Hawk, where Jim is sent to school; later he goes to Lincoln to attend the state university. . . . The story of Jim Burden is the story of Willa Cather: the hero's spiritual and intellectual growth is manifestly the author's own.[21]

Although the superficial similarities between Cather's life and Jim Burden's cited by Hinz are present, it is perhaps not quite right to conclude that the "hero's spiritual and intellectual growth is manifestly the author's own." I would like to contend that far from being Cather's mouthpiece, Jim Burden is her vehicle for criticizing conventional notions regarding women. The conventions that Jim represents are contradicted by Antonia, a strong, independent woman who works out her destiny in defiance of the narrator's expectations.

Jim's very first act of prefixing the possessive adjective "My" to his title, reveals him to be a conventional person conforming to the cultural norms of his society. In fact it determines the entire course of his romance with Antonia. The novel is his account of all that Antonia means to him, or rather, of his attempt to make her "anything that a woman can be to a man."[22]

Right from childhood Jim is conscious of belonging to the privileged sex. Although Antonia is four years older than him, he resents her "protecting manner" (43) because she is a girl and he is a boy. Soon after, he succeeds in winning her respect and admiration by killing an old, lazy rattlesnake. But even Jim realizes that this "dragon-slaying" episode is in reality "a mock adventure; the game . . . fixed . . . by chance, as . . . for many a dragon slayer." (49-50) He had been adequately armed by Russian Peter and the snake was old and lazy. Thus his accolade was unearned. Yet it gave him the feeling of superiority over Antonia that was so essential to him.

Even as a girl, Antonia is characterized by her vitality and an independent spirit. She is "as bright as a new dollar" (4) with skin "a glow of rich, dark colour" and hair that is "curly and wild-looking." (23) She is always on the move: running up a hill, chattering in Czech and broken English, asking rapid questions and struggling to adapt herself to a new environment. Antonia not only wants to learn everything, she also has "opinions about everything." (30) Neither indolent like Lena Lingard nor passive like her sister Yulka, Antonia is "breathless and excited," (35) generous, interested and affectionate. She has no qualms about doing heavy work in the fields and by the time she is fifteen years old, she is a "strong young girl," with her "arms and throat . . . burned as brown as a sailor's." (122) She proudly declares that she "can work like man now" and "help make this land one good farm." (123) Unconcerned about conventions or the criticism levied against her, she emphatically states: "'Oh, better I like to work out-of-doors than in a house!' . . . 'I not care that your grandmother say it makes me like a man. I like to be like a man.' She would toss her head and ask me to feel the muscles swell in her brown arm." (138)

On the other hand, Jim is not very different from Black Hawk's young men of position whom he derides because they cannot have more than a "jolly frolic" with the country girls. In fact, he constantly tries to remake Antonia in the image of the anaemic "daughters of well-to-do families" (198) who embody the town's ideal of womanhood. Disturbed and somewhat threatened by Antonia's pride in her "manly" strength and taste for outdoor work, Jim aligns himself with his grandmother in an effort to "save" Antonia from "chores a girl ought not to do." (126) Jean Schwind in her perceptive analysis of the relationship between Jim and Antonia, comments: "As Jim sees it, Antonia's claim to a 'man's' work is more than a violation of Black Hawk's sense of propriety: it is a violation of human nature."[23] Repeatedly he warns Antonia that heavy field work will "spoil" (125) her, and attempts to subdue the "strong independent nature" that distinguishes her from the other girls of the town. Although it was Antonia's independence that attracted Jim to her in the first place, he is somewhat repulsed by the way she eats with noisy relish "like a man" (125) rather than with ladylike delicacy; and he is disturbed by the beads of perspiration that gather on Antonia's upper lip "like a little moustache" (138) as she picks vegetables with him in the garden. He ridicules the notions of "refined femininity that consider physical exercise rather inelegant for the daughters of well-to-do families." Nevertheless, he worries that Antonia is losing the "nice ways" (125) that distinguish ladies from labourers. In short, Jim's affection for Antonia is conditional. He is proud of Antonia when he believes her to be "like Snow-White in the fairy tale, . . . still 'fairest of them all'" (215); he turns from her when she asserts her individuality.

E.K. Brown in his biography of Willa Cather writes: "At the very center of his [Jim's] relation with Antonia there is an emptiness where the strongest emotion might have been expected to gather."[24] Jim himself admits many years later that at one time he had been very much in love with Antonia. Yet the relationship does not develop. The reason for this I believe to be Jim's ambivalent attitude to Antonia which has been noted above. Attracted to her because of her vitality and strong individuality, he is yet repelled by certain manifestations of it. Similarly, aware of her strong physical appeal, he would yet like her to conform to his ideal to chaste, pure womanhood. And so, when she rebuffs his perfunctory attempt to kiss her, he is proud of her and carries his head high. "her warm, sweet face, her kind arms, and the true heart in her; she was, oh, she was still my Antonia!" (225) He is content to find solace in dreams about Lena Lingard and vainly hopes that he would "have this flattering dream about Antonia." (226)

This reading also helps to explain his reaction to Antonia after Cutter's attempted rape of Jim whom he mistakes for Antonia. Wick Cutter, an old, notorious lecher, returns in the middle of the night to assault Antonia, but meanwhile persuaded by his grandmother's and Antonia's suspicions, Jim has taken her place in bed. He becomes an innocent victim of Cutter's lust and fury at deception. Vile as the Cutter episode is, Jim's nausea seems an overreaction, intensified by his shrill rhetoric and unmodulated tone. Unlike the snake episode, this encounter offers no rewards. It simply reduces him to "a battered object," (249) his body pommeled, his face swollen. His only recognition will be the laughter of the "old man at the drugstore." (250) And he is furious with Antonia: "I heard Antonia sobbing outside my door, but I asked grandmother to send her away. I felt that I never wanted to see her again. I hated her almost as much as I hated Cutter. She had let me in for all this disgustingness." (250) He is furious and disgusted with Antonia because of the overt sexual implications of the incident. His desire to perceive Antonia as an asexual person conflicts with the reality and he hates her for having shattered his illusions.

Unlike Jim's, Antonia's affection for him is not conditional. His rejection of her after the Cutter episode does not in any way diminish her fondness for him. However, abandoned by him, she turns to Larry Donovan and lavishes her affection upon him. A passenger conductor, Larry was "one of those train-crew aristocrats who are always afraid that someone may ask them to put up a car-window, and who, if requested to perform such a menial service, silently point to the button that calls the porter." (304) Usually cold and distant with men, with all women "he had a silent, grave familiarity, a special handshake, accompanied by a significant, deliberate look." (304) He took women into his confidence, shared with them the secret of his unappreciated worth, and always succeeded in making "some foolish heart ache over it." (305) Antonia also falls a victim to his charms and refuses to "hear a word against him." (268) Kind and generous to a fault, Antonia's failing is that "if she once likes people, she won't hear anything against them." (268) Even after she gets an inklng of the fact that he probably has no intention of marrying her, her independent spirit will not allow her to coerce him into marrying her. She tells Mrs. Steavens: "'I thought if he saw how well I could do for him, he'd want to stay with me'." (313) And when he deserts her without marrying her, she is not ashamed of the child but loves it "as dearly as if she'd had a ring on her finger,." (318) and proudly has "its picture on exhibition at the town photographer's, in a great gilt frame." (303) In this part of the novel "The Pioneer Woman's Story," Jim is relegated to the position of the tale recorder, and Widow Steavens, who attended Antonia, is made the narrator. She relates her story with understanding and sympathy and provides a woman's account of a woman's experience, something that Jim is incapable of doing.

When Jim first hears of this event in Antonia's life, his reaction is characteristic: "I tried to shut Antonia out of my mind. I was bitterly disappointed in her. I could not forgive her for becoming an object of pity"; "I could forgive her, . .

if she hadn't thrown herself on such a cheap sort of fellow." (298, 304) This event, like the Wick Cutter incident, taints Antonia as a sexual being and so Jim tries to shut it out of his mind. This is the time when Antonia, abandoned by Donovan, needs Jim most, but he fails to rise to the occasion. Instead of marrying her, all he does is to passionately aver: "'. . . since I've been away, I think of you more often than of anyone else in this part of the world. I'd have liked to have you for a sweetheart, or a wife, or my mother or my sister anything that a woman can be to a man. The idea of you is a part of my mind; you influence my likes and dislikes, all my tastes, hundreds of times when I don't realize it. You really area a part of me.'" (321) Thereupon he leaves, abandoning her to a life of hardship on her brother's farm with an empty, and ultimately broken promise to return soon.

Jim is too weak to marry Antonia or someone like her. He takes recourse to a conventional marriage with a woman who is "temperamentally incapable of enthusiasm," and to playing the sterile role of husband to a woman who offers none of the rich intimacy of a true marriage. His childless marriage is in direct contrast to Antonia's. For Antonia does not allow misfortunes to bow her down. Her life bears testimony to the triumph of the pioneer woman who has achieved victory over her own hard early life and over the forces of nature which make farming in Nebraska an immense struggle. When Jim finally visits her twenty years later she is "a stalwart, brown woman, flat-chested, her curly brown hair a little grizzled." (331) But she "had not lost the fire of life." (336) Although she is a "battered" woman now, and not a lovely girl, she still has "that something which fires the imagination." (353) She could "still stop one's breath for a moment by a look or gesture that somehow revealed the meaning in common things. She had only to stand in the orchard, to put her hand on a little crab tree and look up at the apples, to make you feel the goodness of planting and tending and harvesting at last. All the strong things of her heart came out in her body that had been so tireless in serving generous emotions." (353) Her husband, Anton Cuzak, is at heart a city man, yet Antonia "had managed to hold him here on a farm, in one of the loneliest countries in the world." (366) Surrounded by her large brood of children, she appears to be "a rich mine of life, like the founders of early races." (353) She has certainly fulfilled her special mission in life and is presented almost like an Earth Mother. It is possible to argue that the Earth Mother can be a limiting stereotype. However, as Sharon O'Brien points out "the image of woman as possessing mythic powers of fertility and nurturance could be interpreted as Cather's re-claiming and reworking of a male-perpetuated stereotype which she uses to enhance rather than limit woman's dignity and stature."[25] For Jim, whose personal life has been such a failure, there is nothing to look forward to. All he can do is to look back on the past, with wistful regret. Only memories are left of "the precious, the incommunicable past" that he and Antonia possessed together.

In *A Lost Lady*, Cather once again drew her material from her childhood memories of Nebraska. Marian Forrester, the central figure of the novel, is a direct portrait of Mrs. Garber, wife of Governor Garber whom Willa Cather had known as a child. As in *My Antonia*, the action is seen through the eyes of a young boy, growing up in the West. Niel Herbert is almost Jim Burden renamed, even to being from the South. However, the important difference is that whereas in *My Antonia* the story is told in the first person, in this novel Cather uses the third person narrative technique. Although the story is largely filtered through Niel's eyes and his consciousness provides the controlling perspective, yet the third person narrative method facilitates the introduction of an ironic perspective to offset the limited view of the male protagonist. The double perspective created by the third person narrator—that is, Niel's viewpoint circumscribed by an omniscient narrator—allows Cather to provide a critique of the existing society.

The setting of the novel is a small town in Nebraska, Sweet Water, and the time is the sunset of the pioneer era. Young Niel Herbert is the nephew of the town's leading lawyer, Judge Pommeroy. A proud, handsome youth, at the age of nineteen Niel "lived with monastic cleanliness and severity."

and is characterized by a "reserve which did not come from embarrassment or vanity, but from a critical habit of mind, [which] made him seem older than he was, and a little cold."[26] An avid reader of the classics, especially the *Heroides* which he considers to be "the most glowing love stories ever told," (81) he is an extremely idealistic person. Moreover, his notion of femininity is an abstract and rigid aesthetic based on vague notions of gentility and a pioneer civilization in the most conventional sense. He glorifies the pioneer era in the person of Captain Forrester, the aging pioneer, and his beautiful, young wife, Marian. His first encounter with Mrs. Forrester takes place when he is a young boy of twelve. Having fallen down in the Forrester place and broken his arm, he is carried inside the house where Marian Forrester, the "lovely lady," (28) tends to him for a short while. To his youthful eyes, she appears to belong "to a different world from any he had ever known." (42) Throughout the novel, he persists in judging her according to his own abstract ideal of womanhood which conflicts with reality, and is highly conventional.

Marian Forrester, the woman Niel idealizes, contradicts the conventions represented by Niel and works out her destiny in defiance of his expectations. She also contradicts the social conventions of Sweet Water, represented by the Molly Beasleys who forage through her house and who see only material objects which they reduce to items for barter. Twenty-five years younger than her husband, Captain Forrester, she was brought as a bride by him to Sweet Water where she became well known as a hostess. Cather criticizes the cultural myths which assign to women the position of objects and restrict them to immanence. She does this not only through the character of Niel Herbert, but of Captain Forrester as well. As a wife Marian is an object to be adorned, admired and cherished. It gratified the Captain to have his friends admire his fine stock and his charming wife. She gives him identity: he is remembered as the man "with the beautiful wife," (121) and she provides a means by which he may display his success. For example, the gems she wears represent her husband's "archaic ideas about jewels; . . . They must be costly; they must show that he was able to buy them and that she was worthy to wear them." (51-52) Most of all, she transforms her husband's domain by creating an atmosphere of calm, timelessness, and absolute security.

For Niel, Mrs. Forrester embodied vivacity, vitality and charm.

> Where Mrs. Forrester was, dullness was impossible, he believed. The charm of her conversation was not so much in what she said, though she was often witty, but in the quick recognition of her eyes, in the living quality of her voice itself. One could talk with her about the most trivial things, and go away with a high sense of elation. The secret of it, he supposed, was that she couldn't help being interested in people, even very commonplace people. (70)

According to him she creates the effect of transcending time: "you seem always the same to me, Mrs. Forrester. . . . Just lovely." (39) Although she grows older physically, she gives the impression of remaining constantly young. When Niel returns to Sweet Water after an absence, he notes: "she was older. In the brilliant sun of the afternoon one saw that her skin was no longer like white lilacs,—it has the ivory tint of gardenias that have just begun to fade. The coil of blue-black hair seemed more than ever too heavy for her head. There were lines,—something strained about the corners of her mouth that used not to be there." (112) Yet again, she transforms reality: "But the astonishing thing was how these changes could vanish in a moment, be utterly wiped out in a flash of personality, and one forgot everything about her except herself." (112) Sensitive as Niel is to Marian's charm and personality, he nonetheless cannot conceive of her as a separate entity, an independent individual. Idealizing the conventional view of woman as a wife, he can think of and admire her only in relation to her husband. "Curiously enough, it was as Captain Forrester's wife that she most interested Niel, and it was in relation to her husband that he most admired her. Given her other charming attributes, her comprehension of a man like the railroad-builder, her loyalty to him, stamped her more than anything else. That, he felt, was quality; something that could never become worn or shabby; steel of Damascus." (78) What really fascinates him is her loyalty to a husband who is twenty-five years her senior, and for whose sake she is living a secluded life in Sweet Water, when with all her youth and beauty she could have led a much more interesting life elsewhere. "He sometimes thought of the life she might have lived ever since he had known her,—and the one she had chosen to live. From that disparity, he believed, came the subtlest thrill of her fascination. She mocked outrageously at the proprieties she observed, and inherited thc magic of contradictions." (79)

As Niel persists in viewing Marian Forrester as he would like her to be, he is blind to her relationship with Frank Ellinger, a handsome bachelor of forty years who lives in Denver. The scene in which Ellinger is first introduced to the reader is an example of Cather differentiating her viewpoint from that of Niel. Throughout this scene we learn far more about Niel's reaction to Ellinger than about Ellinger himself. Niel "knew nothing bad about him, but he felt something evil." (46) Yet to guard against our reacting against Ellinger simply as Niel does, Cather makes his character ambiguous. Ellinger had a wild youth, yet "All the while he was making a scandalous chronicle for himself, young Ellinger had been devotedly caring for an invalid mother" (50) and even after his mother's death, he continued to keep her house. Like Marian Forrester, Frank Ellinger infuses life into a scene. When he enters the Forresters' parlour, "suddenly everyone became more lively; the air warmed and the lamplight seemed to brighten." (45) By linking Ellinger to Mrs. Forrester in this way, Cather testifies to the latter's youth and guards against the reader's associating her, as Niel does, too rigidly with Captain Forrester, who is approaching death.

As Niel totally insulates himself from reality, knowledge of Mrs. Forrester's liaison with Ellinger comes as a profound shock to him. On an impulse, he goes up to the Forrester place early one morning and makes "a bouquet for a lovely lady; a bouquet gathered off the cheeks of morning . . . these roses, only half awake, in the defencelessness of utter beauty." (85) He decides to leave them outside one of the French windows so that when she opened the shutters to let in the light, she would find them, and "they would perhaps give her a sudden distaste for coarse worldlings like Frank Ellinger." (85) Just as he was in the act of bending to place the flowers on the sill, "he heard from within a woman's soft laughter; impatient, indulgent, teasing, eager. Then another laugh, very different, a man's. And it was fat and lazy,—ended in something like a yawn." (36) Unable to accommodate sexuality in his imaginative conception of her, Niel draws back in bitter disillusionment. Cather writes: "In that instant between stooping to the window-sill and rising, he had lost one of the most beautiful things in his life. This day saw the end of that admiration and loyalty that had been like a bloom on his existence." (86) In bitterness he mutters "lilies that fester smell far worse than weeds." (87) Cather makes it clear that Niel's reaction results from the fact that Marian Forrester has violated his conception of her. "It was not a moral scruple she had outraged, but an aesthetic ideal." (87)

In explicit contrast to Niel's insistence that Mrs. Forrester be judged according to an abstract aesthetic ideal, is Captain Forrester's judgement of his wife. Here he represents a norm for judgement, a corrective to Niel's perspective. This role is suggested early in the novel, when Niel wonders how much Captain Forrester knows about his wife's involvement with Frank Ellinger. Cather calls Niel's bitter condemnation into question by offering the criterion of Captain Forrester, the representative of pioneer values and the husband involved. "Niel had often wondered just how much the Captain knew. Now, as he went down the hill, he felt sure that he knew everything; more than anyone else; all there was to know about Marian Forrester." (117) Finally, as he lives with the Forresters during the Captain's last days, he perceives the value that accompanies this knowledge: "The longer Niel was with Captain Forrester in those peaceful closing days of his life, the more he felt that the Captain knew his wife better even than she knew herself; and that, knowing her, he—to use one of his own expressions,—valued her." (142-43)

Soon after Niel learns of Mrs. Forrester's relationship with Frank Ellinger, the Forresters suffer a setback in their fortunes. The failure of a Denver bank of which Captain Forrester was the President leaves them in a bad financial position. With this the Captain suffers a stroke and is almost bed-ridden. He seems to accept the reversal in their fortunes and offers no resistance. With the change in their fortunes, Frank Ellinger deserts Marian Forrester. He "plays safe" and marries Constance Ogden from whom he receives a large sum of money. In spite of all these setbacks, Mrs. Forrester struggles against the psychological, emotional and economic deprivations that seem to be inescapable in Sweet Water. With great practical sense and foresight, she realizes that the age of the pioneers is past and that it is essential to come to terms with the present situation. This means that instead of scorning people like Ivy Peters (an upstart yet shrewd young shyster lawyer), it is essential to get along with them. Unlike her husband, she is not willing to submit to defeat and death. As she tells Niel: "Perhaps people think I've settled down to grow old gracefully, but I've not. I feel such a power to live in me, Niel." (125) She spends all her time plotting and scheming as to how to get out of Sweet Water, the town over which an aura of death and defeat lingers.

Throughout this period Marian Forrester's need for human support is contrasted with Niel's critical distance. As she increasingly suffers the effects of economic and physical change, so she looks to Niel for help and support. Upon seeing him, after he had been absent from Sweet Water for two years, she tells him of how much she had looked forward to his visit, saying: "Every night for weeks . . . I've said to myself, 'Niel is coming home, there's that to look forward to'," (111) and then looks at him with "her rarest smile, one he had seldom seen on her face, but always remembered,—a smile without archness, without gaiety, full of affection and wistfully sad.

And the same thing was in her voice when she spoke these quiet words,—the sudden quietness of deep feeling." (114) Yet Niel continues to regard her as an abstract ideal. He envisions her "like a bird caught in a net," and wishes "he could rescue her and carry her off like this,— off the earth of sad, inevitable periods, away from age, weariness, adverse fortune!" (110) Despite this poetic wish to carry her off the earth, Niel offers little actual support during this period. Of course he could not have rescued her from hardships by marrying her the way in which Jim could have rescued Antonia. In this novel, Cather rules out the possibility of a relationship that could have ended in marriage by making the female protagonist, Marian Forrester, much older than the male, Niel Herbert. However, he could have prevented her from falling into the clutches of people like Ivy Peters, if he had extended active support and help to her. Instead, he stays away from the Foresters because he is "irritated" and "annoyed" (118) at the appearance of Ivy Peters so often about the place, and hence "did not go over as often as he had intended" (118) to see the Forresters.

Niel Herbert continues to judge Marian Forrester in terms of his own abstract and conventional view of womanhood. He censures her because, after the Captain's death "she was not willing to immolate herself, like the widow of all these men, and die with the pioneer period to which she belonged; that she preferred life on any terms." (169) This period of bitter questioning climaxes in Niel's seeing Mrs. Forrester with Ivy Peters, after which his bitterness changes to "weary contempt." (169) The irony of Niel's condemnation of Mrs. Forrester is that according to him she "belongs" only to the past. A generation younger than her husband, she actually belongs not to the past but to the present. She refuses to define herself in terms of death and insists that she relates to life, to youth. And so she befriends the young men of the town because she hates "to see them growing up like savages, when all they need is a civilized house to come to, and a woman to give them a few hints." (155) At the dinner party she gives for these young men, her struggle against the dehumanizing economic and cultural forces is vividly portrayed. In spite of the fact that "her eyes were hollow with fatigue, and she looked pinched and worn as he had never seen her," (161) she has the ability to radiate life and charm. She has an effect upon the boys, who "were genuinely moved" (166) by the story she narrates, and upon Niel, who recognizes her potential constancy: "She had, after all, not changed so much since then. . . . She was still her indomitable self, going through her old part . . ." (166-167)

Yet Niel holds it against her that she refuses to limit herself to the past, and so makes "the final break with everything that had been dear to him in his boyhood." (168) According to him, without her husband "she was like a ship without ballast, driven hither and thither by every wind. . . . She seemed to have lost her faculty of discrimination; her power of easily and graciously keeping everyone in his proper place." (152-53) After discovering her intimacy with Ivy Peters, Niel "crossed the bridge in the evening light, 'for the last time.' And it was even so; he never went up the poplar-bordered road again." (170)

It has often been argued that Cather created Marian Forrester as a stereotype of nineteenth century genteel femininity in order that she should stand for a civilized ideal. John Randall echoes J.W. Krutch, Alfred Kazin and Henry Steele Commager, when he argues that "promiscuity becomes a symbol of social degeneration. This equating of the chastity of woman with the moral integrity of a civilization provides the fundamental metaphor upon which the book is based."[27] However, these critics fail to note that this equation is made by Niel Herbert, whose viewpoint Cather undercuts throughout the novel and who is not a reliable narrator. It is Niel who views Marian Forrester in terms of the cultural myths about woman as bearer of culture and moral values. But Cather gives her female protagonist the strength to break through the conventional roles imposed upon her, and to live her own life on her own terms. The last scene of the novel testifies to this. We are told that Marian Forrester is remarried to an Englishman, Mr. Collins who is not only extremely wealthy, but "the kindest of husbands." (174) When Niel hears of this many years later, he is glad that she had "come up again." (174) and that she was well cared for to the end. He is no longer bitter towards her. Rather, he considers it his good fortune to have known someone who "had always the power of suggesting things much lovelier than herself, as the perfume of a single flower may call up the whole sweetness of spring." (172) Even though he considers it fortunate that Marian Forrester "had had a hand in breaking him into life," (171) there is no suggestion that he has changed his conventional views regarding women. Niel Herbert, like Jim Burden before him, is unable to overcome the inherited prejudices regarding women. Niel's inability to transcend the traditional bounds of the society is responsible for the hardships Marian Forrester has to undergo, and for the break up of a relationship that could have been very fruitful.

IV

Willa Cather has generally been regarded as an elegist of the West, specifically Nebraska. It is true that an emotional and imaginative response to Nebraska is at the heart of Willa Cather's fiction, and that the West did provide the raw material for almost all her fiction. However, to see her as merely a celebrator of the pioneer era in the West would be too restrictive. She was greatly concerned about the lot of women, especially the confining and limiting roles imposed upon them by society. In her fiction, she gave expression to this concern by drawing vivid portraits of strong and independent women. As the foregoing discussion of the novels included in this chapter amply shows, these women are not victims, but victors. Even after being betrayed by their male counterparts, they look for alternate modes of fulfillment and invariably succeed in their endeavors. The male protagonists on the other hand are almost diminutive in comparison. They are weak, confused and vacillating, and fail to live up to the expectations of the women. Attracted to the heroines because of their vitality and independence of spirit, they nevertheless view them from a conventional and idealistic perspective of womanhood. Inevitably, they fail the female protagonists at the crucial moment and so the relationship ends unsatisfactorily.

Unlike Glasgow, Cather does not ridicule or satirize her male protagonists. Nor does she depict them as villains. Yet she presents them critically and unsympathetically. As the preceding discussion shows, it is only by closely scrutinizing the texts that the negative aspects of these characters are revealed. With great subtlety and with effective use of irony the author distances her viewpoint from that of her male characters, and shows them up to be essentially confused and tradition-bound. They are almost overshadowed by their female counterparts, with the result that our conventional expectations of a dominating male figure and a subordinate female figure in a work of fiction are belied. However, despite the fact that they are highly inefficacious characters, the male protagonists are by no means artistic failures. The stereotypical views that these male characters have regarding women were commonly held by men in the society in which Cather lived. In her own life Cather had rebelled against the confining roles imposed on women. Fred Ottenburg, Jim Burden and Niel Herbert resemble men as Cather perceived them in real life. She consciously created male characters who are such conventional and ineffectual beings because she could not conceive of them in any other terms. But to see them as only negative portraits through whom the author is presenting a critique of the cultural myths regarding women would be too restrictive a reading. On probing deeper it becomes apparent that Cather clearly meant to convey something more through these "heroes" who are so unheroic in almost every sense of the term. She meant to suggest an ideal image of man, one who would be devoid of the negative traits that her male protagonists exhibit. Such an ideal being would be able to transcend the conventional views of the society and not perceive women in terms of the existing cultural myths. He would thus be able to accept morally and intellectually emancipated women, and women who are achievement-oriented. This would result in a man-woman relationship based on equality and mutual understanding, and acceptance of each other's needs and aspirations—the kind of a relationship that Thea Kronborg at one time believed she could have with Fred Ottenburg. Thus, through her fiction, Cather provides us with the bases on which a successful man-woman relationship can be built.

NOTES

1. Edith Lewis, *Willa Cather Living—A Personal Record* (New York: Alfred A. Knopf, 1953), p. 13.
2. Barbara Bonham, *Willa Cather* (New York: Chilton Book Company, 1970), p. 27.
3. James Woodress, *Willa Cather: Her Life and Art* (New York: Western Publishing Company, 1970), pp. 176.
4. Sandra M. Gilbert and Susan Gubar, *The Madwoman in the Attic: The Woman Writer and the Nineteenth Century Literary Imagination* (New Haven and London: Yale University Press, 1979), p. 50.
5. Woodress, p. 86.
6. Deborah G. Lambert, "The Defeat of a Hero: Autonomy and Sexuality in *My Antonia*," *American Literature*, 53 (1982), p. 676.
7. Elizabeth Shepley Sergeant, *Willa Cather A Memoir* (Lincoln: University of Nebraska Press, 1953), pp. 115-16. Cather had become a great friend of Sarah Orne Jewett shortly before the latter's death in 1909.
8. Woodress, p. 13.
9. J.J. Murphy, "Willa Cather: The Widening Gyre," in J.J. Murphy, ed., *Five Essays on Willa Cather: The Merrrimack Symposium* (Massachusetts: Merrimack College, North Andover, 1974), p. 67.
10. Woodress, p. 132.
11. Carl Van Doren, "Willa Cather," in James Schroeter, ed., *Willa Cather and Her Critics* (New York: Cornell University Press, 1967), p. 14.
12. Susan J. Rosowski, "Willa Cather's Women," *Studies in American Fiction*, 9 (1981), p. 261.

13. Jennifer Bailey, "The Dangers of Femininity in Willa Cather's Fiction," *Journal of American Studies*, 16 (1982), 396.
14. Woodress, pp. 87-88.
15. John H. Randall III, *The Landscape and the Looking Glass: Willa Cather's Search for Value* (Boston: Houghton Mifflin Company, 1960), p. 95.
16. Willa Cather, "Preface to *The Song of the Lark*" (1932; rpt. Boston: Houghton Mifflin Company, 1983), p. 2.
17. Willia Cather, *The Song of the Lark* (1915; rpt. Boston: Houghton Mifflin Company, 1983), p. 334. All further references to the book will be to this edition and shall be incorporated in the text.
18. E.K. Brown, *Willa Cather: A Critical Biography* (New York: Alfred A. Knopf, 1953), p. 205.
19. Brown, p. 199.
20. Woodress, p. 174.
21. John P. Hinz, "Willa Cather—Prairie Spring," *The Prairie Schooner*, 23 (1949), 87.
22. Willa Cather, *My Antonia* (Boston: Houghton Mifflin Company, 1918) p. 321. All further refererces to the book will be to this edition and shall be incorporated in the text.
23. Jean Schwind, "The Benda Illustrations to *My Antonia*: Cather's 'Silent' Supplement to Jim Burden's Narrative," *Publications of the Modern Language Association*, 100 (1985), p. 59.
24. Brown, p. 202.
25. Sharon O'Brien, "Mothers, Daughters and the 'Art Necessity': Willa Cather and the Creative Process," in Fritz Fleischmann, ed., *American Novelists Revisited: Essays in Feminist Criticism* (Boston, Massachusetts: G.K. Hall, 1982), p. 267.
26. Willa Cather, *A Lost Lady* (1923; rpt. New York: Random House, 1972), pp. 33-34. All further references to the book will be to this edition and shall be incorporated in the text.
27. John R. Randall III, p. 180. See also J.W. Krutch, "The Lady as Artist," Alfred Kazin, "Willa Cather," and Henry Steele Commager, "Willa Cather," all rpt. in Schroeter, ed., *Willa Cather and Her Critics*.

Conclusion

It is many decades since Edith Wharton, Ellen Glasgow and Willa Cather disappeared from the literary and cultural scene of America. But, in death, far more tellingly than in life, they have continued to shape the consciousness of our times.

Although during their life time, all the three writers received their fair share of critical acclaim and popularity, some important aspects of their writing received little or no attention. For some years after their death, they were more or less ignored by the critics. About two decades ago, with the advent of feminist critics on the scene, works by women writers were subjected to a careful re-examination. These scholars, interested in describing a female literary tradition different from that of men, have discovered hitherto unexplored and hidden aspects of the works of these writers. Further, they have established the fact that women write out of a distinctively female perspective of experience, or what is often termed as the "female sensibility." Thus, when works by women writers are considered collectively, a recurrence of certain patterns, themes, problems and images can be traced from generation to generation.

Studies by feminist scholars have led to a reevaluation of the works of women writers. What has been discovered is that since these writers wrote out of a different perspective of experience, the criterion for judgement should also be different. Earlier critics and readers failed to properly interpret and appreciate women's writings because they were ignorant of women's values and conceptions of the world. For example, an unbiased reading of Wharton would reveal the fact that she was attempting a different picture of society than James ever dreamed of and that she must therefore be judged in the light of what she attempted and not what a famous contemporary declared his aims to be.

This study has attempted to show that in the works of the three women novelists included in the study, an imaginative representation of man may be found which is related to the distinctive inner life of a woman. Wharton, Glasgow and Cather consistently created weak, convention-bound male protagonists who are juxtaposed against strong, independent and unconventional female protagonists. The male protagonists are unable to live up to the expectations of the female protagonists with the result that in none of these novels do we find a satisfactory and viable man-woman relationship. Earlier critics were of the opinion that these writers' inability to portray strong male protagonists and successful man-woman relationships constituted a weakness in their art. In the recent years, the feminist readings of these novels have generally been concerned with the portrayal of the female protagonists. When the male protagonists have been considered, it has been only to delineate their negative characteristics and to note that they are weak and unheroic. A close and detailed analysis of these novels reveals that the question as to why these novelists consistently created weak male characters is a complex one and cannot be simply dismissed as an artistic limitation on the part of these writers. Their portrayal of negative male protagonists was intentional and part of a conscious design. Unable to conceive of heroes who would be able to overcome the conventional limits of society, the characters they created resemble men as they saw around them in real life. Moreover, through these negative portraits, these writers suggest their ideal image of man.

A reading of Edith Wharton's fiction reveals that not only is Lawrence Selden a "negative hero," but so are John Amherst, George Darrow and Newland Archer. In *The House of Mirth*, Lawrence Selden's inconsistencies, vacillations, cowardice and finally double standards of sexual morality prevent him from giving to Lily Bart the support and understanding that she needs in her struggle to break through the conventional roles that society imposed upon women. As compared to Selden, John Amherst the hero of *The Fruit of the Tree*, is a more dynamic personality with stronger determination. Although he claims to have advanced views on life, he is revealed to be essentially conventional in his perceptions of women. Adhering to the belief that women are supposed to minister to the needs of men and should remain subservient, he is unable to accept the fact that Justine can act independently, and not feel morally bound to report her actions to him. George Darrow, the least attractive of Wharton's male protagonists included in this study, has very little to recommend him. A dilettante like Selden, he is totally smug and complacent about his conventional views regarding women. His utter selfishness and his double standards of sexual morality are largely responsible for wrecking the life and happiness of Sophy Viner, an independent, achievement-oriented young woman. Newland Archer, the male protagonist of *The Age of Innocence* is perhaps the most positive of the negative heroes discussed in this chapter. Although he is unable to transcend the double standards of sexual morality and the conventional views regarding women, at times he at least realizes that by forsaking Ellen Olenska, he has missed something important in life.

All the four protagonists have certain traits in common. Distinguished from those around them by their superior intelligence and a degree of seeming unconventionality which enables them to attract strong and independent young women, they still fail to live up to the expectations of these women. The heroines of these novels, Lily Bart, Justine Brent, Sophy Viner and Ellen Olenska are young women who are trying to break out of the conventional role of womanhood. In their struggle to attain independence and wholeness, they look to their male counterparts for support and understanding. The male protagonists pay lip service to the emancipation of women, but at the crucial moment they fail to live upto the unconventional views they have earlier espoused. This is because at the decisive moment they are unable to overcome the inherited biases in their views of women. As the study has shown, with the exception of Amherst, all of them subscribe to double standards of sexual morality which proves to be a major obstacle in their relationship with the women. The desire to mould the heroines according to their own concept of womanhood is another factor which contributes to the unsatisfactory relationships. Moreover, each one of them has internalized the society's concept which categorizes women into "good" and "bad" so that when they meet an exceptional young woman whom it is not possible to place in either "category," their reactions are extremely ambivalent. However, insofar as she does depict her male protagonists as trying to overcome the obstacles, she does by implication indicate those positive qualities which her ideal man would possess.

A study of the same theme in Ellen Glasgow's fiction yields similar results. Jason Greylock is almost despicable in his weakness. He gets involved with Dorinda when he is already engaged to Geneva. Moreover, he has the effrontery to expect Dorinda to carry on the relationship even though he is married. What he does not know till much later is that Dorinda is one of those rare women who will not allow a broken affair to ruin their life. She looks for an alternate mode of fulfillment and finds it in reclaiming her father's farm and becoming the most successful farmer in that part of the country. In *The Romantic Comedians* Glasgow gives vent to her wrath, and seeks to puncture and punish the vanity of the patriarchal male through the characterization of Judge Gamaliel Honeywell. Her ironic sense of the disparity existing between the conventional views that men have regarding women, and the reality (which gives rise to serious problems in man-woman relationships), is given effective expression in this novel. In addition, she satirizes the double standards that allow a man to fall in love even with one foot in the grave, but debar a woman from giving expression to her emotional needs.

The Sheltered Life is the most somber of Glasgow's tragicomedies of manners. Once again Glasgow criticizes the society that sanctions philandering on the part of men and offers no career options for women. George Birdsong's "roving nature'' negates his many likable qualities and is responsible for wrecking his wife Eva's life and happiness and, to a certain extent for deflecting Jenny Blair from her chosen path of pursuing a career.

Thus, all the three male protagonists in Ellen Glasgow's novels studied here—Jason Greylock, Gamaliel Honeywell and George Birdsong are most unheroic and are revealed to be weak and ineffectual and subscribe to the prevailing double standards of sexual morality. What Glasgow does is to belie our conventional expectations of a heroic male figure. She presents the reader with a series of male characters who are divested of the aura that generally surrounds the heroes of fictional works. They are reduced in stature, but they are by no means artistic failures. Writing out of a distinctively female experience of reality, Glasgow consciously created her male characters as weak and ineffectual beings. They resemble men as she saw around her in real life. In the society in which Glasgow lived and about which she wrote, characters like Judge Honeywell and George Birdsong were commonly found. Society not only sanctioned their double standards but almost conspired to foster their polygamous instincts. By satirizing these characters, comically deflating their vanity, and showing them up as essentially ridiculous and weak, the author is certainly expressing her dissatisfaction with the patriarchal society which creates such norms. But, to look at them as merely weak and satirical portraits, and vehicles of Glasgow's criticism of the patriarchal society, would be too limiting. The author clearly meant to suggest some positive values through these negative portraits. The embodiment of these positive values would perhaps approximate Glasgow's ideal image of man. Such an ideal figure would be endowed with the strength of character the male protagonists of the novels discussed lack so greatly. Further, such an ideal figure would have the courage to honour commitments, and the ability to look critically at the society and to transcend its limiting views. Moreover, an imaginative understanding, on the part of such an ideal figure, of the emotional needs and expectations of women, and of their desire to lead an independent and "whole" life would make possible a successful man-woman relationship.

A close examination of Cather's fiction reveals that in spite of appearances to the contrary, she was deeply concerned about the lot of women and the whole question of man-woman relationship. However, it is rarely that a man-woman relationship is dramatized in her fiction. The reason for this was her strong conviction that achieving women were not likely to find suitable mates and should therefore look for alternate modes of fulfillment. The first novel in which she gave expression to her abiding concern was *The Song of the Lark*, in which she created her memorable artist heroine, Thea Kronborg, who is strongly achievement-oriented. As has been shown in the foregoing chapter, Fred Ottenburg, the male protagonist, has many qualities that make him an attractive and agreeable suitor, but he lacks the most essential ones. Although he prides himself on his advanced views on life, he has internalized the society's concept of womanhood to a large extent. For example, he believes that artists and professionally inclined women are not the "marrying kind." Further, like many of Wharton and Glasgow heroes, he considers it a male prerogative to have extramarital relationships and imagines that unconventional women like Thea would readily accede to such liaisons. In *My Antonia*, Jim Burden, the male protagonist as well as the narrator, not only admires Antonia, a strong and heroic woman, but is also fascinated by her. However, his inability to transcend conventional views about women makes his attitude towards Antonia somewhat ambivalent and prevents his relationship with her from becoming a fruitful and satisfactory one. Similarly, Niel Herbert, the young protagonist of *A Lost Lady* is unable to overcome the inherited biases regarding women. Like Jim Burden, he repeatedly tries to re-make Marian Forrester according to his idealistic perception of womanhood. This makes him largely responsible for the hardships that Marian faces, and for the break-up of a relationship which could have been beneficial to both. In the last analysis, all the three men are revealed to be weak, confused and essentially conventional, failing the heroines of the novels at the crucial moment. However, the fact that these male protagonists are so unheroic and that there are no satisfactory man-woman relationships in these novels is not indicative of any failure on Cather's part. The creation of weak male protagonists is intentional and these characters are real and authentic insofar as they resemble men as Cather perceived them in real life.

Edith Wharton, Ellen Glasgow and Willa Cather grew to creative maturity in an age when to be a woman and a writer was considered to be an anomaly. All three faced great hostility in their life time and each one of them rebelled in her own way against the confining roles that society imposed upon women. Having faced similar problems as women aspiring to be writers in a patriarchal society, it is almost inevitable that their fiction should reveal some likenesses. It is in their treatment of the male protagonists and the man-woman relationship that this similarity is most apparent. Wharton generally wrote about the New York elite society, Glasgow about the Southern aristocracy and Cather about the pioneering West. Hence, the setting of their novels differs greatly. But, there is not much difference in their portrayal of the male protagonists and the man-woman relationship. In none of the novels included in this study do we find a satisfactory and viable man-woman relationship. A major factor responsible for this is the subscription of the male protagonists to double standards of sexual morality. Their inability to accept and understand the ambitions of achievement-oriented women, and the emotional needs of women, is another factor which contributes to an unsatisfactory relationship. Moreover, almost all the male protagonists tend to regard their female counterparts as beings whom they can remake according to their own concept of womanhood. Thus the male protagonists of these writers are inherently flawed and significantly limited.

In spite of strong similarities in their treatment of the male protagonists and the man-woman relationship, the three novelists differ from one another in some noteworthy respects. For example, Wharton's heroes are generally endowed with intelligence and a degree of unconventionality. They are also shown as trying to overcome the inherited biases regarding women. Their interaction with the independent young heroines does have an impact on them, though it does not lead to any self-realization, or a greater understanding of their female counterparts. On the other hand, Glasgow's heroes have hardly any qualities to recommend them. Almost contemptible in their weakness and smugness, they do not even make an effort to overcome the stereotypical view of womanhood and to understand the aspirations of the heroines. They are thoroughly encapsulated in their own conventional views of life, and coming into contact with strong and independent women has no significant effect on them. Cather's depiction of the male protagonists resembles that of Wharton in some respects. Fred Ottenburg has many traits in common with a Wharton hero—intelligence and a degree of unconventionality. Jim Burden and Niel Herbert are also invested with a certain amount of intellectual prowess. Although attracted to unconventional and strong women, both Jim and Niel are revealed to be almost escapists and cowards in their desire to avoid any mature relationship with these women. Yet, they are not as despicably weak as Glasgow's heroes. Glasgow satirized, ridiculed and mocked her male protagonists. On the other hand, Wharton and Cather distance their viewpoint from that of their male protagonists by effective and subtle use of irony. Cather's use of it is so subtle that a cursory reading of *My Antonia* and *A Lost Lady* often gives the impression that Jim Burden and Niel Herbert are the author's spokesmen.

Men's perceptions of women, and how women relate to their inner lives, has been portrayed in literature down the ages. Edith Wharton, Ellen Glasgow and Willa Cather were among the first American novelists to express women's perceptions of men, and their concept of an ideal male figure. Pioneers in the field, their work has significant bearing on our understanding of not only the socio-cultural milieu of that time, but of the psyche of women as well. Women's hitherto unexpressed desires, their unfulfilled expectations, and their dissatisfaction with the existing social, cultural and economic conditions are given admirable expression in their novels. In the years intervening between the time when these writers lived and wrote and the present day, the situation of women has changed a great deal, and by and large, for the better. The women's liberation movement has not only improved the lot of women in some fundamental respects, but has also changed the concept of womanhood to a certain extent. No longer are reading, writing and thinking considered to be alien to the female self. Novelists like this change. Through the vision they create of fulfilling relationship that can exist between liberated women and men, their writings clearly indicate the immense advantages that would accrue from the emancipation of women, which would inevitably lead to the liberation of men. As Betty Friedan put it: "Perhaps men may live longer in America when women carry more of the burden of the battle with the world, instead of being a burden themselves." A Justine Brent could well shoulder half the responsibilities of a John Amherst (which she does till the break in their relationship) in his struggle to bring about social and industrial reform. A relationship in which each partner can realize the full human potential, and in which there is mutual understanding and respect, is certainly an ideal worth aspiring for. Thus, insofar as each of these writers indicates the parameters on which a viable man-woman relationship can be based, they are visionaries and have relevance in the present times.

Selected Bibliography

Primary Sources

Cather, Willa. *A Lost Lady*, 1923; rpt. New York: Random House, 1972.

______. *My Antonia*. Boston: Houghton Mifflin Company, 1918.

______, *The Song of the Lark*. 1916; rpt. Boston: Houghton Mifflin Company, 1983.

Glasgow, Ellen. *Barren Ground*. 1925, 1933; rpt. New York: Hill and Wang, 1968.

______, *A Certain Measure: An Interpretation of Prose Fiction*. New York: Harcourt, Brace and Company, 1938.

______, "The Novel in the South." *Haper's Magazine*, 158 (1928), 93-100.

______. *The Romantic Comedians*. New York: A.L. Burt Company, 1926.

______, *The Sheltered Life*, 1938; rpt. New York: Hill and Wang, 1979.

______, *The Woman Within*. New York: Harcourt, Brace and Company, 1954.

Wharton, Edith. *The Age of Innocence*, 1920; rpt. New York. Charles Scribner's Sons, 1970.

______. *A Backward Glance*, 1933; rpt. New York, Charles Scribner's Sons, 1964.

______. *The Fruit of the Tree*. 1907; rpt. London: Virago Press, 1984.

______. *The House of Mirth*. 1905; rpt. New York: Charles Scribner's Sons, 1969.

______. *The Reef*. 1912; rpt. New York: Charles Scribner's Sons, 1965.

______. *The Writing of Fiction*. New York: Charles Scribner's Sons, 1925.

Secondary Sources

Abel, Elizabeth, "Introduction," *Writing and Sexual Difference*. Ed. Elizabeth Abel. Chicago: University of Chicago Press, 1982, pp. 1-7.

Ammons, Elizabeth. "The Business of Marriage in Edith Wharton's *The Custom of the Country*," *Criticism*, 16 (1974), 326-338.

______. *Edith Wharton' Argument with America*. Athens: University of Georgia Press, 1980.

______. "The Engineer as Cultural Hero and Willa Cather's First Novel." *American Quarterly*, 38 (1986), 746-760.

Anderson, Hilton. "Edith Wharton as Fictional Heroine." *South Atlantic Quarterly*, 69 (1970). 118-123.

Aristotle. *Politics, The Basic Works of Aristotle*, ed. Richard McKeon. New York: Random House, 1941.

Auchincloss, Louis. *Edith Wharton: A Woman in Her Time*. New York: The Viking Press, 1971.

______. *Ellen Glasgow*. Minneapolis: University of Minnesota Press, 1964.

______. *Pioneers and Caretakers: A Study of Nine American Women Novelists*. Minneapolis: University of Minnesota Press, 1961, pp. 20-122.

Auerbach, Nina. "Feminist Criticism Reviewed." *Women and Literature*, 1, Special Number on "Gender and Literary Voice." Ed. Janet Todd, 1980, pp. 258-268.

Bailey Jennifer. "The Dangers of Femininity in Willa Cather's Fiction." *Journal of American Studies*, 16 (1982), 391-406.

Baldwin, Alice M. "Ellen Glasgow," *South Atlantic Quarterly*, 54 (1955), 394-404.

Beach, Joseph Warren, *The Twentieth Century Novel*. New York: Appleton Century Crofts, 1932.

Beauvoir, Simone de. *The Second Sex*. 1949. rpt. Penguin Books, 1984.

Becker, Allen W. "Ellen Glasgow's Social History." *Texas Studies in English*. 36 (1957), 12-19.

______. "Ellen Glasgow and the Southern Literary Tradition." *Modern Fiction Studies*. 5 (1959-60), 295-303.

Bell, Millicent. "Edith Wharton and Henry James: The Literary Relations." *PMLA*, 74 (1959), 519-637.

Bendixen, Alfred and Zilversmit Annettee, ed. *Edith Wharton: New Critical Essays*. New York: Garland Publishing, 1962.

Bennett, Mildred R. "The Childhood Worlds of Willa Cather." *Great Plains Quarterly*, 2 (1982), 204-209.

______. "Willa Cather's Bodies for Ghosts." *Western American Literature*, 17 (1982), 39-52.

Bevilacqua, W.F. ed. *Fiction by American Women: Recent Views*. New York: Associated Faculty Press, 1983.

Bloom, Edward A and Lillian D. Bloom. *Willa Cather's Gift for Sympathy*. Illinois: Southern Illinois University Press, 1962.

Bloom, Lillian D. "On Daring to Look Back with Wharton and Cather." *Novel*, 10 (1976), 167-178.

Bodkin, Maud. *Archetypal Patterns in Poetry*. 1934; rpt. London: Oxford University Press, 1965.

Bond, Tonette L. "Pastoral Transformations in *Barren Ground*." *Mississippi Quarterly: The Journal of Southern Culture*. 32 (1979), 565-576.

Bonham, Barbara. *Willa Cather*. New York: Chilton Book Company, 1970.

Bristol, Marie. "Life Among the Ungentle Genteel: Edith Wharton's *The House of Mirth Revisited*." *Western Humanities Review*, 16 (1962), 371-374.

Brooks, Van Wyck. *The Confident Years*, 1885-1915. New York: Alfred A. Knopf, 1953.

Brown E.K. *Willa Cather: A Critical Biography*. New York: Alfred A. Knopf, 1953.

Brown, Muriel "Growth and Development of the Artist: Willa Cather's *My Antonia*." *Midwest Quarterly*, 33 (1991), 93-107.

Buchan, Alexander M. "Edith Wharton and 'The Elusive Bright Winged Thing.'" *New England Quarterly*, 37 (1964).

Burch, Beth. "Willa Cather's *A Lost Lady*: Woodpecker and Marian Forrester." *Notes on Contemporary Literature*, 11. 4 (1981), 7-10.

Caldwell, Ellen M. "Ellen Glasgow and the Southern Agrarians." *American Literature*, 56 (1984), 203-213.

Canby, Henry Seidel, "Willa Cather (1876-1947)." *Saturday Rev. of Literature*, 30, 19 (May 10, 1947), 22-24.

Candido, Joseph, "Edith Wharton's Final Alterations of *The Age of Innocence*." *Studies in American Fiction*, 6 (1978), 21-31.

Carlin, Deborah. *Cather, Canon and the Politics of Reading*. Amherst: The Univ of Massachusetts Press, 1992.

Charles, Sister Peter Damian. "*My Antonia*: A Dark Dimension." *Western Quarterly Review*, V (1929),187-198.

Clark, Emily. "Appreciation of Ellen Glasgow and Her Work." *Western American Literature*, 2 (1967), 91-108.

Coolidge, Olivia. *Edith Wharton*. New York: Charles Scribner's Sons, 1964.

Cross, Wilbur. "Edith Wharton." *Bookman*, 63 (August 1926), 641-46.

Dahl, Curtis. "Edith Wharton's *The House of Mirth:* Sermon on a Text." *Modern Fiction Studies*, 21 (1975-76), 572-76.

Daiches, David. *Willa Cather: A Critical Introduction*. New York: Cornell University Press, 1951.

Davidson, Cathy N. "Kept Women in *The House of Mirth.*" *Markham Review*, 9 (1979), 10-13.

Dimock, Wai-Chee. "Debasing Exchange: Edith Wharton's *The House of Mirth.*" *PMLA*, 100 (1985), 783-792.

Donovan, Josephine. *After the Fall: The Demeter-Persephone Myth in Wharton, Cather, and Glasgow*. University Park and London: The Pennsylvania State University Press, 1989.

Ellmann, Mary. "Manners, Morals and Mrs. Wharton." *Southern Review*, 84 (1976), 526-32.

______. *Thinking about Women*. New York: Harcourt, Brace and Company, 1968.

Epstein, Joseph. "Willa Cather: Listing toward Lesbos." *The New Criterion*, 2 (1983), 35-43.

Erlich, Gloria C. *The Sexual Education of Edith Wharton*. California: Univ. of California Press, 1992.

Fetterley, Judith. "'The Temptation to be a Beautiful Object': Double Standard and Double Bind in *The House of Mirth.*" *Studies in American Fiction*, 5 (1977), 199-211.

Field, Louise M. *Ellen Glasgow: Novelist of the Old and New South*. New York: Doubleday, Page and Company, 1923.

Freadman, Anne. "Introduction." "Forum: Feminism and Interpretation Theory." *Southern Review*, 16 (1983), 149-73.

Friedan, Betty. *The Feminine Mystique*, 1963; rpt. Penguin Books, 1971.

______. *The Second Stage*. New York: Summit Books, 1981.

Fryer, Judith. "Cather's Felicitous Space." *Prairie Schooner*, 55 (1981), 185-198.

Gardiner, Judith Kegan, "On Female Identity and Writing by Women." *Writing and Sexual Difference*. Ed. Elizabeth Abel. Chicago: University of Chicago Press, 1982, pp. 177-191.

Gargano, James. "'The House of Mirth': Social Futility and Faith." *American Literature*, 44 (1972), 137-143.

Geismar, Maxwell. *The Last of the Provincials: American Novel, 1915-1925*. New York: Hill and Wang, 1943, pp. 153-222.

______. *Rebels and Ancestors: The American Novel, 1890-1915*. Boston: Houghton Mifflin Company, 1953, pp. 219-283.

Gelfant, Blanche H. "The Forgotten Reaping Hook: Sex in *My Antonia*," *American Literature*, 43 (1971), 60-82.

Gerber, Philip L. "Willa Cather and the Big Red Rock." *College English*, 19 (1958), 152-157.

Giannone Richard. *Music in Willa Cather's Fiction*. Lincoln: University of Nebraska Press, 1963.

Gilbert, Sandra M. and Susan Gubar. *The Madwoman in the Attic: The Woman Writer and the Nineteenth Century Literary Imagination*. New Haven and London: Yale University Press, 1979.

Glazier, Lyle. *Decadence and Rebirth: Hacetepe Lectures in American Literature*. Hacetepe University Press, 1971.

Godbold, Stanly E. Jr. *Ellen Glasgow and the Woman Within*. Baton Rouge: Louisiana State University Press, 1982.

Gorham, Deborah. *The Victorian Girl and the Feminine Ideal*. Bloomington: Indiana University Press, 1982.

Gornick, Vivian. *Essays in Feminism*. New York: Harper and Row, 1978.

Greene, George. "Willa Cather's Grand Manan." *Prairie Schooner*, 55 (1981), 233-240.

Hamblen, Abigail Ann. "Edith Wharton in New England." *New England Quarterly*, 38 (1965), 239-244.

Harris, Richard C. "Renaissance Pastoral Conventions and the Ending of *My Antonia*." *Markham Review*, 8 (1978), 8-11.

Heilbrun, Carolyn G. "A Response to Writing and Sexual Difference," Ed. Elizabeth Abel. Chicago: University of Chicago Press, 1982, pp. 291-297.

Helmick, Evelyn Thomas, "Myth in the Works of Willa Cather." *American Studies* (Kansas), 9, 2 (1968), 63-69.

Hicks, Granville. "The Case Against Willa Cather." *The English Journal*, 22 (1933), 703-710.

Hinz, John. "Willa Cather—Prairie Spring." *Prairie Schooner*, 23 (1949), 82-88.

Holman, C. Hugh. "April in Queenborough: Ellen Glasgow's Comedies of Manners." *The Sewanee Review*, 82 (1974), 263-283.

Hopkins, Viola. "The Ordering Style of 'The Age of Innocence.'" *American Literature*, 30 (1958), 345-57.

Howe, Irving ed. *Edith Wharton: A Collection of Critical Essays*. Englewood Cliffs, New Jersey: Prentice Hall, 1962.

Huf, Linda. *A Portrait of the Artist as a Young Woman: The Writer as Heroine in American Literature*, New York: Frederick Ungar Publishing Company, 1983.

Inge, M. Thomas, ed. *Ellen Glasgow: Centennial Essays*. Virginia: University Press of Virginia, 1976.

Jessup, Josephine L. *The Faith of Our Feminists: A Study in the Novels of Edith Wharton, Ellen Glasgow, Willa Cather*. New York: Biblo and Tannen, 1965.

Kazin, Alfred. *On Native Grounds*. New York. Harcourt, Brace and Company, 1942, pp. 73-82; 247-64.

Kolodny, Annette. "Some Notes on Defining a 'Feminist Literary Criticism.'" *Critical Inquiry*, 2 (1975), 75-93.

______. "Dancing Through the Minefield; Some Observations on the Theory, Practice and Politics of a Feminist Literary Criticism," *Feminist Studies*, 6,1 (1980), 1-25.

Lambert, Deborah G. "The Defeat of a Hero: Autonomy and Sexuality in *My Antonia*," *American Literature*, 53 (1982), 679-90.

Lawson, Richard H. *Edith Wharton*. New York: Frederick Ungar Publishing Company, 1977.

Leavis, Q.D. "Henry James's Heiress: The Importance of Edith Wharton." *Scrutiny*, 7 (1938), 26-276. rpt. Irving Howe ed. *Edith Wharton: A Collection of Critical Essays*, pp. 73-88.

Lerner, Gerda, "The Challenge of Women's History." *The Majority Finds Its Past*. New York, 1981.

Lesser, Wayne, "The Problematics of Regionalism and the Dilemma of Glasgow's *Barren Ground*." *Southern Literary Journal*. 11 (1979), 3-21.

Lewis, Edith, *Willa Cather Living—A Personal Record*. New York: Alfred A. Knopf, 1953.

Lewis, R.W.B. *Edith Wharton: A Biography*. New York: Harper and Row, 1975.

Lidoff, Joan. "Another Sleeping Beauty: Narcissism in *The House of Mirth*." *American Quarterly*, 32 (1980), 519-539.

Lovett, Robert Morse. *Edith Wharton*. 1925; rpt. New York: Norwood, 1975.

______. *Portrait of Edith Wharton*. New York: Appleton-Century Company, 1947.

Lyde, Marilyn J. *Edith Wharton: Convention and Morality in the Work of a Novelist*. Norman: University of Oklahoma Press, 1959.

Lynskey, Winifred. "The Heroes of Edith Wharton." *University of Toronto Quarterly*, 23 (1954), 354-61.

Martin, Terence. "The Drama of Memory in *My Antonia*." *PMLA*, 84 (1969), 304-11.

Mason, J. "An Interesting Willa Cather Letter," *American Literature*, 58 (1986), 109-111.

Maxwell, D.E.S. *American Fiction: The Intellectual Background*. New York: Columbia University Press, 1963.

McDowell, F.P.W. *Ellen Glasgow and the Ironic Art of Fiction*. Madison: University of Wisconsin Press, 1963.

McDowell, Margaret B. *Edith Wharton*. Boston: Twayne Publishers, 1976.

______. "Viewing the Custom of her Country: Edith Wharton's Feminism." *Contemporary Literature*, 15 (1974), 521-538.

McManis, Jo Agnew. "Edith Wharton's Hymns to Respectability." *The Southern Review*, 7 (1971), 986-993.

Meeker, Richard K. "The Shadowy Stories of Ellen Glasgow." *The Dilemma of the Southern Writer*. Virginia: Longwood College, 1961, pp. 95-117.

Miller, James E. Jr. "*My Antonia*: A Frontier Drama of Time." *American Quarterly*, 10 (1958), 476-484.

Millet, Kate. *Sexual Politics*. London: Rupert Hart-Davis, 1970.

Morgan, William W. "Feminism and Literary Study: A Reply to Annette Kolodny." *Critical Inquiry*, 2 (1976), 807-816.

Moseley, Ann. "The Dual Nature of Art in *The Song of the Lark*." *Western American Literature*, 14 (1979), 19-32.

Murphy, John J. ed. *Five Essays on Willa Cather: The Merrimack Symposium*. Massachusetts: Merrimack College, North Andover.

Murphy, John J., "Filters, Portraits, and History's Mixed Bag: *A Lost Lady* and *The Age of Innocence*." *Twentieth Century Literature*, 38 (1992), 476-485.

Murr, Judy Smith. "History in *Barren Ground* and Vein of Iron: Theory, Structure and Symbol." *The Southern Literary Journal*, 8 (1975), 39-54.

Nevius, Blake. *Edith Wharton: A Study of Her Fiction*. Berkeley: University of California Press, 1961.

Oates, Joyce Carol. "Is there a Female Voice? Joyce Carol Oates Replies." *Women and Literature*, 1, Special Number on "Gender and Literary Voice." Ed. Janet Todd, 1980, pp. 10-11.

O'Brien, Sharon, "Mothers, Daughters and the 'Art Necessity': Willa Cather and the Creative Process." *American Novelists Revisited: Essays in Feminist Criticism*. Boston: G.K. Hall, 1982.

Plante, Patricia R. "Edith Wharton and the Invading Goths." *Midcontinent American Studies Journal*, 5, 2 (1964), 18-23.

Pratt, Annis. *Archetypal Patterns in Women's Fiction*. Bloomington: Indiana University Press, 1981.

______. *The New Feminist Criticism. College English*, 32 (1971), 872-78.

______. "Women and Nature in Modern Fiction." *Contemporary Literature*, 13 (1972), 476-490.

Rainwater, Catherine. "Narration as Pragmatism in Ellen Glasgow's *Barren Ground*." *American Literature*, 63 (1991), 664-82.

Raper, J.R. *From the Sunken Garden: The Fiction of Ellen Glasgow*. Baton Rouge: Louisiana State University Press, 1980.

______. "Glasgow's Psychology of Deceptions and *The Sheltered Life*." *The Southern Literary Journal*, 8 (1975), 27-54.

Robinson, Lilian S. "Dwelling in Decencies: Radical Criticism and the Feminist Perspective." *College English*, 32 (1971), 879-89.

Romines, Ann. "After the Christmas Tree: Willa Cather and Domestic Ritual." *American Literature*, 60 (1988), 61-82.

Rosowski, Susan J. "The Pattern of Willa Cather's Novels." *Western American Literature*, 15 (1981), 243-63.

______. "Willa Cather: A Pioneer in Art: *O Pioneers and My Antonia*." *Prairie Schooner*, 55 (1981),141-154.

______. "Willa Cather's Women." *Studies in American Fiction*, 9 (1981), 261-75.

______. "Writing Against Silences: Female Adolescent Development in the Novels of Willa Cather." *Studies in the Novel*, 21 (1989), 60-77.

Rubin, Larry, "Aspects of Naturalism in Four Novels by Edith Wharton." *Twentieth Century Literature*, 2 (1957), 182-91.

Rubin, Louis D. *No Place on Earth*. Austin: University of Texas Press, 1959.

Rouse, Blair. *Ellen Glasgow*. New York: Twayne Publishers, 1962.

Santas, Joan Foster. *Ellen Glasgow's American Dream*. Charlottesville: University Press of Virginia, 1965.

Scholes, Robert E. "Hope and Memory in *My Antonia.*" *Shenandoah*, 14 (1962), 24-29.

Schriber, Mary Suzanne. "Edith Wharton and Travel Writing as Self-Discovery." *American Literature*, 59 (1987), 257-67.

Schoeter, James, ed. *Willa Cather and Her Critics*. New York: Cornell University Press, 1967.

Schwind, Jean. "The Benda Illustrations to i: Cather's 'Silent' Supplement to Jim Burden's Narrative." *PMLA*, 100 (1985), 51-67.

Scura, Dorothy Mc Innis, ed. "Special Section: *Barren Ground*, Ellen Glasgow's Critical Arrival." *Mississippi Quarterly*, 32 (1979), 549-609.

Sergeant, Elizabeth Shepley. *Willa Cather: A Memoir*. Lincoln: University of Nebraska Press, 1963,

Sharma, O.P. "Feminist Image in the Novels of Ellen Glasgow: The Early Phase." *The Research Bulletin*. Panjab University, No. 40, 1968.

Shaw, Patrick W. "*My Antonia*: Emergence and Authorial Revelations." *American Literature*, 56 (1984), 527-540.

Showalter, Elaine. "Feminist Criticism in the Wilderness." *Writing and Sexual Difference*. Ed. Elizabeth Abel. Chicago: University of Chicago Press, 1982, pp. 9-35.

Slote, Bernice, ed. *The Kingdom of Art: Willa Cather's First Principles and Critical Statements*. Lincoln: University Nebraska Press, 1966.

Spector, Judith A. "Gender Studies: New Directions for Feminist Criticism." *College English*, 43 (1961), 374-378.

Stein, Allen F. "Wharton's Blithedale: A New Reading of *The Fruit of the Tree*." *American Literary Realism*, 12 (1979), 330-37.

Stegner, Wallace, "Willa Cather's *My Antonia.*" *The Voice of America Forum Lectures. The American Novel Series*, 13.

Stewart, Grace. *A New Mythos: The Novel of the Artist as Heroine 1877-1977*. Vermont: Eden Press Women's Publications, 1981.

Stone, Grace, "Ellen Glasgow and her Novels." *Sewanee Review*, 50 (1942), 289-301.

Stouck, David, "Marriage and Friendship in *My Antonia.*" *Great Plains Quarterly*, 2 (1982), 224-231.

______. *Willa Cather's Imagination*. Lincoln: University of Nebraska Press, 1975.

______. "Women Writers in the Mainstream: A Review Essay." *Texas Studies in Literature and Language*, 20 (1978), 660-69.

Thiebaux, Marcelle, *Ellen Glasgow*. New York: Frederick Ungar Publishing Company, 1982.

Tintner, Adeline R. "Jamesian Structures in *The Age of Innocence* and Related Stories." *Twentieth Century Literature*, 26 (1980), 332-47.

Todd, Janet. "Introduction." Women and Literature, 1. Special Number on "Gender and Literary Voice." Ed. Janet Todd. 1980, pp. 1-9.

Trilling, Diana. "The House of Mirth Revisited." *Harper's Bazaar*, 81 (1947), 126-27.

Tuttleton, James W. "Leisure, Wealth and Luxury: Edith Wharton's Old New York." *Midwest Qudrterly*, 7 (1966), 337-52.

Voloshin, Beverly. "A Historical Note on Women's Fiction: A Reply to Annette Kolodny." *Critical Inquiry*, 2 (1976), 817-820.

Waid, Candace. *Edith Wharton's Letters from the Underworld: Fictions of Women and Writing*. Chapel Hill: Univ. of North Carolina Press, 1991.

Wagenknecht, Edward. *Cavalcade of the American Novel.* Calcutta: Oxford and IBH Publishing Company, 1969.

______. "Willa Cather." *Sewanee Review*, 37 (1929), 221-239.

Wagner, Linda M. "*Barren Ground*'s Vein of Iron: Dorinda Oakley and Some Concepts of the Heroine in 1925." *Mississippi Quarterly*, 32 (1979), 553-64.

______. *Ellen Glasgow: Beyond Convention*. Austin: University of Texas Press, 1982.

Walton, Geoffrey. *Edith Wharton: A Critical Interpretation.* Teaneck: Fairleigh Dickinson University Press, 1982.

Wershoven, Carol. *The Female Intruder in the Novels of Edith Wharton*. London: Associated University Presses, 1982.

Whipple, T.K. *Spokesmen: Modern Writers and American Life*. New York: Appleton, 1922.

White Jr. George L. "Willa Cather." *Sewanee Review*. 50 (1942), 18-25.

Wilson, James Southall. "Ellen Glasgow's Autobiography." *Virginia Quarterly Review*. 31 (1955), 292-298.

Wittenberg, Judith B. "The Critical Fortunes of *Barren Ground. The Mississippi Quarterly*, 32 (1979), 592-607.

Wolff, Cynthia Griffin. *A Feast of Words: The Triumph of Edith Wharton*. New York: Oxford University Press, 1977.

______. "Lily Bart and the Beautiful Death." *American Literature*, 46 (1974), 16-40.

______. "A Mirror for Men: Stereotypes of Women in Literature." *Massachusetts Review*, 13 (1972), 205-219.

Woodress, James. "The Uses of Biography: The Case of Willa Cather." *Great Plains Quarterly*, 2 (1982), 195-203.

______. "Willa Cather: Her Life and Art." New York: Western Publishing Company, 1970.

Woolf, Virginia. *A Room of One's Own*. 1929; rpt. Grafton Books, 1985.

Worby, Diana Zacharia. "The Ambiguity of Edith Wharton's 'Lurking Feminism.'" *Mid-Hudson Language Studies*, 5 (1982).

Younge, Patricia Lee. "*A Lost Lady*: The End of the First Cycle." *Western American Literature*, 7, 1 (1972), 3-12.

______. "Willa Cather's Aristocrats." *Southern Humanities Review*, 14 (1980), 43-56, 111-25.

Zlotnik, Jan. "The Virgin and the Dynamo: A Study of the Woman as Hero in the Novels of Edith Wharton, Ellen Glasgow and Willa Cather." *DAI*, 38: 878A-79A, 1978.